MURDEROUS INTENT

A COLLECTION OF MURDERS IN BUCKINGHAMSHIRE

LEN WOODLEY

Book Castle PUBLISHING

TO IAN

By the same author
Murder in Buckinghamshire
Buckinghamshire Murders
Deadly Deeds - A compilation of Buckinghamshire murder cases
The Last Patrol – Policemen killed on duty while serving in the Thames Valley
A History of the Chipping Norton Borough Police 1836 – 1857

First published November 2009 by
Book Castle Publishing
2a Sycamore Business Park
Copt Hewick
North Yorkshire HG4 5DF

ISBN 978 1 903747 95 7

Designed and typeset by Tracey Moren, Moren Associates Limited
www.morenassociates.co.uk
Printed by TJ International in Great Britain.

Front cover picture: Pistol used in murder (see chapter ten)

CONTENTS

ABOUT THE AUTHOR

Len Woodley was born at Slough and on leaving school joined what was then Buckinghamshire Constabulary, which later was amalgamated into the Thames Valley Police. He served for over thirty years before retiring and then worked for the High Sheriff of Buckinghamshire and for British Waterways as a Patrol Officer.

Now fully retired he researches the story of policing within the Thames Valley Police area, as well as old murders. He is also a member of the Police History Society.

INTRODUCTION

Murder has been with us since the beginning of time, of course. The earliest recorded murder is when Cain slew Abel, a case of fratricide. And people have been killing ever since. Murder has been recorded in the county of Buckingham since people could write and there have been reports of murders being committed in the seventeenth, eighteenth and nineteenth centuries and earlier, as can be found from the first chapter in this book. With the increase in population over the years, murder has become, unfortunately, commonplace and we, the public, are, as our ancestors were, still very much interested in the subject. Witness the almost daily instances which are recorded in newspapers, television and radio, as well as documentaries and dramas which also appear before us almost nightly.

So I present to you a number of murders that occurred within Buckinghamshire, committed for an extraordinary variety of reasons.

SOURCES

BOOKS
'And so to Bath' by Cecil Roberts, 1940
'A Short History of the Berkshire Constabulary 1856 – 1956' by W. Indge, 1956
'Tour of the Grand Junction Canal' by J. Hassell, 1819
'A History of Milton Keynes' (2 volumes) by Sir Frank Markham, 1976

NEWSPAPERS
Bucks Gazette, Windsor, Slough & Eton Express, Slough Observer, Bucks Free Press, Bucks Examiner, Bucks Herald, Buckingham Advertiser.

ACKNOWLEDGEMENTS
I have to thank many people for their help in the preparation of this book and for the time they spent assisting me with my enquiries. They were Derek Edmonds, Chris Esling, Joan Kidstone, Andrew Carr, Margaret Jelley, Ruby Keenan, John Robinson, John Burt, Keith Milner Q.P.M., the late Malcolm Crabtree, Jill Vallis, Tony Walton, Pat Kenny, Ray Tilley, Mick Shaw, Laurie Ekins, Brian Douglas and, of course, my wife Mary. If I have inadvertently omitted anyone, I beg their forgiveness.

MURDER AT THE OSTRICH

COLNBROOK - 12TH CENTURY

At the south-eastern end of the old county of Buckinghamshire nestles the village of Colnbrook. It was old when the medieval chronicler Froissart related that ambassadors from King Phillip of France, sent to pay homage to the King of England at Windsor in 1337, 'had dyned in the Kinge's chamber and after they departed laye the same night atte Colnbrook'.

In 1440, a vast army camped in the meadows about the village, ready to march on Windsor Castle and replace Henry IV with the deposed King Richard II. Henry, however, escaped to London and raised his own army, so large that it completely intimidated his adversary's.

Of course, Good Queen Bess slept here when, as Princess Elizabeth and a prisoner of Mary Tudor, she was being escorted from Woodstock to Hampton Court and was forced to spend a night at Colnbrook when a wheel came off her coach as it trundled through the village.

During the English Civil War, Prince Rupert and his entourage stayed here prior to venturing forth into battle with the Parliamentarian forces at nearby Brentford. It is said that he spent the night at The Ostrich, one of several old inns in Colnbrook and which is reputed to be the fourth oldest public house in the country, or the third oldest if you choose to believe the plaque on the wall.

Colnbrook flourished again in the eighteenth century when it became fashionable to journey from London to Bath, that renowned spa town, and to rest overnight at either The Ostrich or any of the other inns or taverns that served the passing trade.

1

Travellers would think themselves lucky if they had crossed the notorious Hounslow Heath, the so called 'dreaded heath', and had escaped the attentions of the highwaymen who lurked there hoping to relieve coach passengers of their money and valuables.

The claim to fame or notoriety of The Ostrich, however, belongs further back in history. In the reign of Henry 1 (1100 – 1135), it was the custom of wealthy West Country clothiers to travel to the capital to sell their wares which had been loaded upon the backs of packhorses. On their return they were of course carrying large sums of money about them and were prey to all evil doers on their long way home.

During this period, The Ostrich was kept by one Thomas Jarman and his wife, who gave in to the temptation of robbing their overnight guests

The Ostrich Inn, Colnbrook.

COLNBROOK.—YE OLDE OSTRICH INN

of their money. However, realising that just stealing the merchants' money would soon result in their detection, they resolved that they must also murder their victim, so that there were no witnesses to their wicked crimes.

"Ye Olde Ostrich Inne," Colnbrook, Bucks. Corridor leading to entrance to Blue Room.

Interior of The Ostrich Inn.

Accordingly, they installed in one of the bedrooms, for some reason named the 'Blue Room', a bed fastened over a trapdoor. When, in the middle of the night, the wealthy guest was in the soundest of sleeps, no doubt helped by imbibing the local ale or wine, the bolts would be drawn by the villainous innkeeper and his wife and the hapless victim would then shoot down into a boiling cauldron of water, where he would not only be scalded but drowned! A truly horrible fate! If the absence of the guest was noted the next day, Jarman would reply that he had left without paying his bill.

How many were so despatched it is impossible to know, but matters came to a head when a merchant by the name of Thomas Cole, who regularly stayed at the inn, arrived one night on his way home. Whether he had a presentiment of death or was just depressed is not known, but he arrived at The Ostrich apparently 'in a most melancholy mood'. Jarman's wife sought to alleviate his fears. "Doubt not Master Cole. You are like enough, by the course of nature, to live many years." "God knows," replied the despondent traveller. "I have never found my heart so heavy before." On his last night on earth, Cole's spirits could not even be lifted by some musicians who attended The Ostrich and played to him, seeking to dispel his melancholia, but after a while he tired of them and dismissing them he retired to his bedroom. The Jarmans waited until they were certain that their important guest was sound asleep, then, going downstairs to the kitchen where the boiling cauldron stood, they pulled the bolts and the unfortunate Cole fell from his bed to a ghastly death.

Next morning the evil landlord gave his usual explanation for the merchant's absence from the breakfast table. However, it would appear that Jarman had forgotten the wealthy clothier's horse which had somehow managed to stray from where it had been stabled and which, embarrassingly for the Jarmans, refused to move from their inn. Enquiries were made into the disappearance of Thomas Cole, and the Jarmans sought to escape retribution by flight, but were discovered hiding in Windsor Forest. Both were swiftly tried, convicted and hanged. Jarman, it is reported, confessed to murdering sixty persons in such a brutal fashion.

"Ye Olde Ostrich Inne," Colnbrook, Bucks. Corridor, showing window overlooking Blue Room in which more than 60 murders were committed.

Interior of The Ostrich Inn.

FATHER, DEAR FATHER!

WING - 1837

One Friday in March of 1838, a large number of people crowded the doors of the Assize Court in Aylesbury. When the doors were opened, there was such a rush that the Sheriff's javelin men were pushed aside in the melee that ensued, as the crowd made haste to obtain seats. The court was soon filled by the chattering horde and the Judge, on taking his seat, commented on the noise.

Why had so many people congregated in the Court on that cold March morning? True, it was a murder trial that was about to take place, but that alone could not explain the reason for the number of men and women who attended. Perhaps it was because it was a rather unusual case. Patricide! A man allegedly murdered by his son. That might be one explanation for so many people being there. Or was it because the accused was a mere lad, whose youthfulness appealed to the onlookers, especially the ladies?

One of the local newspapers reported that the prisoner, when 'put up', was a 'juvenile looking personage, though said to be 18 years of age'. Later in the proceedings one witness, who was said to know the family well, said of him "He is a humane youth..." He was William Adams and had been committed by the coroner to the Buckinghamshire Lent Assizes for the wilful murder of Thomas Adams, his father, at Burcott in the parish of Wing on 28th December 1837.

There were apparently nine daughters and two sons in the family. William Adams, the report continued, 'assumed a firm and undaunting appearance and did not appear the least disconcerted at the situation in

6

High Street, Wing – late nineteenth century.

which he was placed, or at all annoyed at being the object of universal interest and observation. In fact he appeared the least concerned of any in the Court, and upon being arraigned gave his plea of 'Not guilty' in a firm manner, and so audibly as to be heard by everyone present'.

After the preliminaries had been gone through, Sergeant Storks, for the prosecution, stood up and addressed the Court. The father of the accused, he said, had been found in a 'cow house' situated on a part of his farm called Fox Covert Hill, lying on his back, with his legs crossed, and the back of his head wounded in such a manner that must have been caused by the shot of a gun. After outlining the case in detail, Sergeant Storks then produced the witnesses for the prosecution. The first presented plans of the farm occupied by Thomas Adams, showing, amongst other things, the cow house where the deceased had been found. A necessary but somewhat tedious piece of evidence for the general public in the galleries of the Court, and their restlessness drew the attention of the Judge.

Matthew Colliar was the first witness of any interest. He had been working on the farm on the afternoon of Friday, 28th December. There had been a group of them working together that day. Between two and three o'clock they had seen William Adams walking towards them carrying a single barrelled shotgun. Colliar had watched him as he veered over to an area known as the Turfmoor, where he shot some larks and then shot at a snipe. After that young William had gone along a brook in the direction of a turnip field and had been lost to the witness' sight. Colliar said that about half an hour later he had heard the report of a gun coming from that field. Then, approximately ten minutes later another shot was heard. Shortly afterwards, between four and five o'clock, he had seen William returning; only this time he was riding a mare, his father's horse. Earlier that afternoon, he had also seen Thomas Adams as he passed by the group of men. This was after the first two shots had been fired.

The next witness, who had been working in the same party as Colliar, corroborated what he had said. John Sharp, who had worked for Thomas Adams for eight years, recalled that the deceased had gone out into the field after having dinner. He had been riding his mare. The accused, Sharp said, had also been at dinner which had been at one o'clock. The next time he had noticed young Mr. Adams had been around four o'clock when he had seen him leading his father's mare into the yard. He had also observed him carrying a gun, which he had taken into the house. He had next seen him leave the house around dusk. When he was cross-examined he stated that he had never known the deceased to stay out in the fields after dark.

George Bone now stepped into the witness box. He was, he announced, the horsekeeper to Thomas Adams and had worked for him since Michaelmas, although he had been employed by him on and off for some years previously. Thinking back to the fatal day, he recalled

8

that he had been carrying dung to a place called the Broad Stitching. As he was coming along the Soulbury Road he had seen his master on his black mare; he never rode any other horse. A little while later he had also seen William Adams in the turnip field, which was several yards away from where he had just seen Thomas Adams. He had seen him fire his gun. Bone had carried on with his work and had not seen William again until he had returned home at dusk. When he was questioned about Thomas Adams' working arrangements, Bone said that Adams had only once started work at dusk and then only for an hour and a half. He had never, in the years that he had worked for Mr. Adams, known him to be so late before or since that occasion.

When William had returned, Bone had asked him if he could go to Leighton Buzzard, the nearest town of any importance, but William had replied that he had been invited out to a psalm singing feast at Wing that night, and that his father would not like them both to be absent. If he, Bone, stayed at home that night, William had told him, he might let him go to Leighton Buzzard the next evening. William, he recalled, had seemed quite normal when they had held this conversation. The horsekeeper added that William had then said, "I wonder where my father is that he does not come home to have his tea?"

Bone added that after William Adams had returned from the psalm singing feast at about half past eight, he had asked Bone to go out with a Richard Judge and look for his father. After they had been to one or two houses, in case Thomas Adams had been there, William had approached Bone and told him that he and his father had parted at Broad Stitching, which was at the top of Foxhole Turnip, that afternoon. His father had told him that he suspected Bone of taking corn from the New Barn and that he would go and watch to see if Bone was in fact stealing.

The men had then searched the barn where Adams had allegedly told his son that he was going to watch from, but they had found no trace of the old farmer there. They had then visited a neighbour that 'old' Adams, as Bone called him, had said it was his intention to see, but when that person informed them that he had not seen Adams, the search party had returned to Wing. There they had visited all the public houses without success. They had then returned to the farm and looked in the rick-yard and stables but no trace could be found of Thomas Adams.

When he was cross-examined by the defence counsel, Bone said that he had seen William ride his father's mare in hay time and harvest. He also admitted that he had seen other people shooting about the turnip field 'this frost'.

William Judge, an underkeeper to Lord Chesterfield, stated that about four o'clock on 28th December, he had encountered William Adams between Burcott and Wing. Adams had been going in the direction of Wing and Judge had joined him. They had gone to The Queen's Head public house and had drunk two pints of ale. They had moved on to The Cock where they had drunk a glass of rum, all of which had been paid for by William. Judge had then gone home, but had returned to Wing where he saw William in the company of a woman. William had told Judge that he was going to fetch a fiddle to have a dance. William had also told Judge that his father was missing; father and son having parted company that afternoon, Thomas indicating that he was going to the New Barn to watch Bone.

William Adams, William Judge and others had then gone out searching for Thomas Adams. As they were doing so, William had mentioned that he had not fallen out with his father since 1st September that year. He had quarrelled with his father about a gun being loaded with clay, which his father had said he, William, had done on purpose in order to kill him.

After the party had searched some of the buildings on the farm, William had then said, according to the witness, that he thought it was not much use to search any further till morning. However the witness' father persisted, saying that he would look through the cowshed, and break open the door if that was necessary. Judge's father had said that he would go to the cow house and New Barn. When they had reached the cow house there had been a hurdle across the entrance which Mr. Judge senior had removed. He had moved some hay and had looked into the interior where he had seen the body of Thomas Adams. William, on seeing his father lying there, had exclaimed, "Oh my poor father! What shall I do?" He had then fainted. The Judges had taken him home. William, Judge continued, had told him the next day that his father had been in possession of two £5 notes and some sovereigns.

When he was cross-examined, William Judge said that there had been much anxiety about Thomas Adams being missing. He was also asked if the prisoner had showed much reluctance in going to the cow house. "No," replied the witness. "Nor any alteration in him till he saw the body, when he appeared much agitated and fainting."

Richard Judge, the last witness' father, was the next man to give evidence, and the Court listened attentively to the man who had discovered the body of the deceased. He was a gamekeeper, also employed by Lord Chesterfield. He said, "On the evening of the 28th December, the prisoner came to my house at Burcott, and said his father was missing and asked me to help him in searching for him. He said he had left his father at Broad Stitching as he was going to New Barn, and he had sent him home with his mare."

Judge explained that the distance between Broad Stitching and New Barn was between 400 to 500 yards. After giving details of the preliminary search, the witness now reached the crucial part when he and the search party had reached the cow house.

"I saw the hay plainly through the hurdle…I moved the hay and saw the body lying on its back. I moved three trusses of hay that were on the body; I pulled off some hay with my stick and saw his face…We went home to Adams' house and examined the spot the next morning as soon as it was light. It seemed that the deceased's head had fallen out of the cow house; there was blood on the ground about a foot and a half from the threshold covered with clover hay. We took the body home." The witness had not seen any traces of the body having been dragged into the cow house.

After a pause, Richard Judge proceeded to tell the Court that William Adams had left his father eighteen months previously and had stayed with him for a few days. Father and son had apparently quarrelled over a gun. His father said that William had loaded it with clay to kill him; his son denied that he had done so.

When he was under cross-examination, Judge gave more details surrounding the finding of the body. He agreed that the prisoner had shown no reluctance in going to the cow house and had made great exclamations of grief when he saw the body, which had been discovered about eleven thirty that night. The distance, Judge added, from where the blood was found at the threshold to where the body laid was some yards, but he had not seen any marks of dragging the body along. Thomas had been a tall man, he went on, but weighed only about ten stone. His body had been skilfully and carefully covered up. There was a little loose hay over the face and two or three trusses on the body. No money had been found in his pockets, which were open. Only a tobacco box had been found in one of the pockets. Questioned about the deceased's horse, Judge said that it had once been steady if a gun had been fired near her, but lately she was unsteady if she heard the report of a gun.

The next witness was Thomas Worster who said that he had worked for Thomas Adams for seven or eight years. On the day in question he had seen his employer in the turnip field sometime between one and two o'clock. He had also seen the prisoner that afternoon, and they had had some discussion concerning the sheep that Worster was looking after. William had told the witness that, among other things, he had fed the sheep and had put them into the rick-yard; there was no need to go to them. Worster had replied that they would not lie there, whereupon William had moved them to another place.

About eleven o'clock that night, he recounted, William Adams had come to his lodgings and asked him if he had seen his father as he had gone about his work. Worster had replied that he had not seen his father after he had seen father and son, both together in the turnip field. He had next seen the prisoner early the next morning in the kitchen of his employer's house when William had said that there had been a bad accident. On the evening of the following day, the prisoner had come to him and had said that if he could not get someone to swear that they had seen him part with his father at the top of Foxhill, he should be done. "Lord have mercy on me," Worster had exclaimed, "you don't say." The prisoner had then said, "I must go, for the Policemen are after me."

There was then some question as to whether this part of Worster's evidence should be admitted, as he did not appear to have given it at the Coroner's Inquest. He now stated that he had appeared twice before that Court. Worster was questioned about his appearances before the Coroner, but eventually prosecuting counsel withdrew his evidence regarding what Worster had stated Williams Adams had said. (However, the jury could not strike from their minds that particular testimony.)

The Bucks Gazette then reported that Samuel Perkins, a Sergeant of the 'New' (sic) Police at Aylesbury, now gave his evidence (1). On Friday, 29th December he had gone to Burcott about five o'clock and had met the prisoner on the road. William Adams had told him that three guns had been fired off the previous afternoon about four o'clock. When Perkins had spoken to him again, Adams said that he could give no further information in the matter. He had left his father in the cowhouse. His father had told him to take his horse home, as he should go for a walk as he thought it would do him good. He added that he would go to the barn to watch Bone, whom he suspected of taking corn. Sergeant Perkins then told William that he had heard that one shot had been sufficient to do the injury to his father's head. William had responded that he supposed it might.

Sergeant Perkins had next seen him about half an hour later at the door of his house. "I have a witness," William had allegedly told the Police Officer, "to prove that I never fired the gun." "Do you mean the gun that shot your father?" the Sergeant had queried. "Yes!" had been the reply. Sergeant Perkins had then said, "Has anybody accused you?" "No," had been the response, but the Sergeant added that Adams had continued that he thought that the questions the Sergeant had put to him implied that he suspected him.

The Sergeant had invited Adams to take a walk with him. As they strolled together, Perkins asked Adams what time he had left his father. William had replied that it had been about half past three. Sergeant Perkins had then said, "You were the last person with your father. You came home with his horse. You were out with a gun, you had powder and shot and your father is found shot in the cowhouse." The two men had then returned to the farmhouse, having agreed to meet the following morning. The Policeman continued his enquires and had then "resolved to secure him (William) that night." He had not been able to find him, however, and so with others he had gone looking for him. They had gone to a public house in Wing, but he was not there. As they had emerged from the pub, the Policeman had seen two men walking in the direction of Burcott. Sergeant Perkins went after them and they started running away. He had run after them and had overtaken them, grabbing hold of one of them by the collar. It was William Adams! He had said, "I will go with you." The Sergeant had taken him to The Cock at Wing where he had searched him. He found a chequered handkerchief with what he thought was "…much blood." Looking at William's shooting jacket, the Policeman had found that it was bloody too. This the prisoner explained away by saying that it was the blood of a hare he had killed a fortnight previously.

William Adams admitted firing the gun twice on the fatal afternoon when he had shot at a snipe but had not killed it. Sergeant Perkins had asked him if Adams had reloaded his gun after firing it twice. "No," had been the reply. He had not had time to reload it in the cow house. His father and he had dressed the sheep.

When he had been asked about the money his father had been carrying with him, William believed that he had about £60 on him. The Sergeant had duly searched the cow house where he found only a watch.

Mr. Richard Olley, a doctor from Leighton Buzzard, had performed the post mortem on Thomas Adams. He gave a detailed account of the terrible injury inflicted upon the farmer, finding that a gunshot wound to the back of the head had caused death. The gun had been fired close to the deceased's head when it had been discharged.

A Parish Constable of Wing (2), Thomas Windmill, who had assisted Sergeant Perkins, stated that the prisoner, whilst in his custody, asked him if he had been to his house. Windmill said that he had not. Had he seen Worster, he had then been asked. Again the Constable said that he had not. William Adams had then told Windmill that Worster was the man who could clear him, for he was innocent.

FATHER, DEAR FATHER!

Hannah Jordan, who was next to give evidence, said that she had been working on the Adams farm in the spring of 1837, with the prisoner nearby. When he had seen his father approaching them, William Adams had exclaimed, "Yonder he is coming. Damn him, I wish somebody would blow his bloody brains out!" Now, this was strong testimony and Mr Kelly, for the defence, was quick on his feet and elicited from the witness that her husband had been sent to gaol for stealing potatoes belonging to Mr. Adams. This had occurred about two years previously. She denied, however, that she had been accused of stealing bread and cakes from the bakehouse, nor had she ever said of the prisoner that she "…would do for him!"

The next man in the witness box caused a slight sensation. His name was James Fuell and he was a prisoner at Aylesbury gaol, he announced. He had, he revealed, had a conversation with the accused whilst they had been incarcerated together, the previous week. "He said he would tell me the truth of his father's death as far as he knew."

Fuell was by now being listened to attentively by everyone in the Court, eager to hear what the felon had to say. "He said his father accused him of robbing him of £10 and said he would send him to Gaol. He had then told him that some of his father's sheep had the foot rot. The prisoner went to put them in the cow house. His father and he were there together, this was on Thursday in Christmas week. The prisoner had a gun in his hand when he was alone with his father. He went into the cow house and dressed the sheep. His father went to pull some turnips for the sheep. They were leaving the door together to pull the turnips. The prisoner took the gun in his hand, put a cap on it and tried it. He had shot his father in the back part of the neck when he was in the cow house. He then picked him up and took him to the further side of the cow house, laid him on his back and turned the sheep out. When he came back he saw his father move his arm. He loaded his gun again outside. He came back and shot him again in the face. He rifled his pockets, took his pocket book out, covered him over with hay, got on his pony and rode home. When he got home, he wanted to go to the little house, and going along he put the pocket book into the hedge. He

15

went there again next morning, and as he was going along he picked up the pocket book which he put in a hole over the privy and covered it up with a tile. He had eleven sovereigns and a half and the key of a desk in a purse. He kicked a hole with his foot by the dahlia roots and put the purse there and covered it up. He told me all this in course of conversation. It came out by degrees as we were talking together."

This would appear to be fairly damning evidence and defence counsel rose to do his uttermost to destroy any credibility this witness might carry. First of all he was questioned about why he was in Aylesbury Gaol. "I have been in prison five weeks last Sunday on a charge of fowl stealing," Fuell conceded. When asked when and why he had mentioned what William Adams had told him, Fuell replied that it might have been more than a week previously that Adams had confided in him and that he had then informed the turnkey. He had also told the Governor of the Gaol, Mr. Sherriff. "If it could do me any good, it was not my duty to cloak it. It would ease my mind and lighten my own case." Fuell acknowledged, however, that, "A good many folks get clear by giving evidence against others." In respect of his sentence for his offence, Fuell had to admit that he did not expect to receive a sentence of seven years transportation.

Defence counsel had now got the bit between his teeth and prodded the witness as to how many times he had been imprisoned, and Fuell disclosed that it had been four years previously when he had been sentenced to two months in gaol. Then he was forced to confess that he had been in prison four times, or was it five or six or seven? In fact he could not recall how many times he been in prison, nor how old he was when he had first been sentenced. He did remember that one conviction was for cruelty to a dog!

Sergeant Perkins was recalled to the witness box and he stated that he had gone to the privy mentioned in Fuell's evidence and had searched it, and, although he had found a broken tile and two loose ones, he had not found a pocket book.

This concluded the case for the prosecution.

Mr. Kelly for the defence now rose and addressed the jury. In a long speech, which lasted for three hours, he said that one great point raised for the defence was that the report of the two shots heard in the direction of the cow house had been heard on the evening of the day of the murder after five o'clock, and consequently after the prisoner had gone home, according to the testimony given by the prosecution. Thus, he expostulated, this made it possible that Thomas Adams had been done to death by someone other than his son, who could not have fired either of the last two shots.

To prove his point, Mr. Kelly now produced several witnesses to aver that the shots had been fired late in the evening, and therefore after the accused had been seen in Wing. One commented that "… the neighbourhood is greatly infested with poachers and bad characters…" A man, who gave evidence for the defence, stated that he had seen William Adams passing by one day and Hannah Jordan had muttered to him under her breath, "If I live, I'll do him such a kindness as he has done my husband!"

A witness, who knew Fuell, said, "I would not believe him on his oath upon any consideration!"

That concluded the defence case and after addressing the jury on behalf of the prosecution, the Judge then summed up for their benefit. The jury were absent for twenty minutes before bringing in a verdict of 'Not Guilty.' A conclusion which was greeted by loud cheers by the people assembled in the Court, notwithstanding the lateness of the hour; it was by now 4 a.m., and the case had commenced at 9 a.m. the previous morning. As the prisoner left the Court he was again greeted with cheers and went straight to an inn where his friends were waiting, in order to celebrate his release from custody.

The Law was not to be denied, however, and William Adams was promptly re-arrested and charged with the theft of his father's pocket book, which contained several sovereigns and some £5 notes, one on the Bank of England, others on 'country banks'.

At the next Assizes, the case was run through and James Fuel was again produced as the prime witness for the prosecution. Several others came forward to say that they would not trust his word. Despite this, the jury deliberated for only ten minutes this time before returning with a verdict of 'Guilty'.

The Judge urged Adams to use the rest of his days in repentance for his dreadful crimes and his '…obdurate hardness of heart in rifling the bleeding body of his father and heartlessly appropriating the money of that parent'. He regretted that the law only allowed him to pass a sentence of seven years transportation (3) and, had his father been living when the robbery had been committed, the punishment might have been for a longer term.

The murder remains unsolved, and it is a matter of conjecture as to whether William Adams did murder his father, or had some 'person or persons unknown' committed the crime?

(1) Aylesbury had a small police 'force' under the Lighting and Watching Act. There was no County Constabulary at the time.
(2) At this time each parish selected an unpaid constable to serve for a period.
(3) In effect, the passing of a sentence of seven years transportation at this time did not mean that the offender would automatically be sent to Australia. They were removed to the hulks and after a number of years were released, without ever going abroad.

POOR MARY ANN!

THE BURNHAM ABBEY FARM MURDER - 1853

By the mid 1850s Ralph Willis Goodwin, a farmer and butcher, had resided at Burnham Abbey Farm for three years. The farm itself was situated near to the Bath Road, close to the village from which it took its name, and on the site of the ancient Abbey of Burnham. It had only recently been modernised.

Goodwin employed several people both in the house and on the farm. Two of these, Mary Ann Sturgeon, a housekeeper, and Moses Hatto, aged about 23 years, a groom and general servant, lived in the actual farm with Goodwin, whilst others resided at nearby cottages.

Goodwin was a bachelor, and on one or two nights a week rode over to Langley Marish, approximately four miles away, to visit his cousins, the Ives. He would leave shortly after 5 p.m. and return late in the evening. On his return, Hatto, who was under instructions to await his master, would come and take his horse and place it in the stables.

Mary Ann should have been abed by this time, but before she retired for the night, she had to clear up and give Hatto and John Bunce, the bailiff, who lived in a nearby cottage, some supper. She had to place a nightlight and shade in the passage of the house, and then she would go to her bedroom, usually about 10 p.m.

On Tuesday, 1st November 1853, Goodwin left the farm at around 5.30 p.m. and rode over to see the Ives. He left his cousins' place shortly before 11 p.m., arriving back at Burnham Abbey Farm at 11.30 p.m. Upon his arrival at the latter place he tapped on the kitchen window and Moses Hatto responded immediately, coming out and taking Goodwin's

High St, Burnham.

horse from him. Goodwin noticed something strange about his general servant cum groom that night. For some reason Hatto's clothes between his knees and ankles were wet through.

As Hatto took charge of his master's horse, he informed Goodwin that about quarter to eleven he had heard a noise, and fifteen minutes later he had heard it again. He had risen, gone out of the house and had roused John Bunce. The two men went looking, found a loose colt and had tried to catch it; one man going one way around the house whilst the other went a different way. It was as they were trying to secure the animal that Hatto had fallen into some water in the pigsty. During the course of the search, Hatto related to Goodwin that he had called up at Mary Ann's window but she had not replied.

Hatto, having reported this incident, took his master's horse, and Goodwin entered the farmhouse by way of the kitchen door. He found that the door between the kitchen and the passage was fastened and he tried to force it open but could not. Goodwin thought that this was odd as it was usually left open at Mary Ann's request. He went to a front door of the house and let himself in with a latchkey.

The no doubt convivial evening and the ride home in the chilly autumn night air made Goodwin want to go to the water closet and when he emerged he encountered Hatto, who asked him if anything was amiss. Goodwin, mystified by the question, replied that he did not know, whereupon Hatto left and Goodwin went past the kitchen door.

As Goodwin did so, he noticed some spots of grease and blood on the floor matting and some blood on the door skirting. He called out, "Hatto! How's this?"

The groom came running back and, looking down where his master pointed, replied that he did not know. Goodwin shone a light along the floor and discovered a tooth and a bloody hairpin a few feet from the bloodstains. He also pointed this out to Hatto who just shrugged his shoulders.

The bewildered farmer made his way upstairs and, as he reached the landing, he noticed smoke coming from Mary Ann's bedroom. Alarmed, he ran back downstairs, calling out and, whilst Hatto held a bucket, Goodwin pumped some water into it.

Goodwin's next action was to run out of the house and summon Bunce, telling him that the house was on fire and to come and assist him. Goodwin returned to the farmhouse and, with Hatto close behind, the two men entered Mary Ann's bedroom.

They saw a fire in the centre of the room and the bucket of water was thrown over it. Several more were needed before the fire was extinguished, however, and Goodwin's next action was to open one of the windows. As the smoke filled room cleared, Goodwin noticed the body of Mary Ann Sturgeon lying on the floor, and a pitiable sight it was too, for her legs had been badly burnt by the fire, whilst the clothes covering the upper part of her body had been singed. Goodwin also noticed that a table had been broken up and placed on top of her body and had been used as fuel for the fire.

A doctor was sent for and he made a preliminary examination of Mary Ann, stating the rather obvious that the poor woman was quite dead. He had been assailed by the smell as he had entered Mary Ann's bedroom. In his own words at a later hearing he put it that "…he had been overpowered by the smell when he had first effected entry into the room. It was like burnt flesh and fat." Also he had smelled naphtha. The matter, he decided, was one for the Coroner.

The next day a more detailed post mortem examination of the deceased was performed by Dr. Roberts. The body had been badly burned, the doctor observed; when had examined Mary Ann's body, he concluded that it must have taken two hours "… to consume the body with more than ordinary flames." Mary Ann's body, he noticed, was lying across the room with her head close to the jamb of the fireplace. There were wounds to her head which appeared to have been inflicted by a blunt instrument. Dr. Roberts removed the badly charred remains of the table which had been placed on top of the housemaid and gently turned her body over. Her facial features were 'much blackened', he recorded, whilst her nose '...was much beaten'. Her tongue protruded, whilst her face was very much swollen on one side. The blows inflicted to the head of Mary Ann, the doctor decided, had caused her death. There were marks across the back of her left hand and one of the bones in her ring finger had been broken, as if her arm had been raised to protect herself. The severe burning to the body had been carried out after death. Some napkins were found under the head of Mary Ann. Also, a quantity of clothes had been placed under the body as if for the purpose of aiding its burning. The doctor had been shown the tooth which Goodwin had found and he, the doctor, had then fitted it into the socket in the mouth of the deceased.

One thing Doctor Roberts did ascertain was that Mary Ann was not pregnant. Sometime after, in fact the Tuesday week following the death, the doctor observed a bruise on one of Hatto's hands, a week or a fortnight old. He had examined Hatto's hands and conjectured "from the man's statements of his using naphtha that the marks might have been burnt by naphtha."

There was blood about a foot high on the jamb, the doctor noticed. In fact there was a great deal of blood about the room. He also observed that a table had been broken up, the remains were found strewn over the deceased and these were partially burnt.

A poker was found in the fireplace with blood, bone and hair adhering to it. In fact, one of the many Police officers, who had been called in and was nosing about the scene of the murder, had seen it, picked it up and was promptly told by Dr. Roberts to leave it alone! Dr. Roberts thought that this could have been used to beat Mary Ann to death.

Dr. Roberts now looked about the house. He could see that there were bloody fingermarks on top of the banisters with spots of blood on the stairs. There were also large pools of blood on the floor '...nearly as large as a hand', the doctor observed, whilst in a wall in the passage he saw bloodstains, 'as if a hand had smeared it with blood'. Poor Mary Ann had been subjected to a sustained and ferocious attack.

The local Police, as mentioned above, had been summoned. They were John Webb, a parish constable (1), and Daniel Sexton, described as 'the Chief Constable' of Maidenhead (2). Webb examined the farm but could find no sign of anyone breaking into the house. The two Police officers looked over the scene of the murder and both noticed the bloody fingermarks on a piece of wainscoting. When the Coroner, Mr. Charsley, arrived, they drew the attention of the Coroner to them.

Enquiries commenced and John Bunce was interviewed. On the night of the murder, he related that he had gone to bed about 9 o'clock. About 10.30 p.m. he had been roused by his wife, who had been awoken initially by a dog barking. Bunce had looked out of his bedroom window and had heard footsteps. He had called out, "Who's there?" but at first there had been no reply. He had started to dress himself when he heard Hatto call out, "Get up Bunce! I think there is somebody about the place!"

He and Hatto had then looked about the farmhouse and had seen a loose colt and the two men had shut it in. They had then gone into the yard and he had heard Hatto call to him that he had fallen in a puddle and he was covered in 'dunghill water'. When Bunce had gone to him, Hatto had held up his hands remarking, "See what a mess I'm in."

Bunce remarked that he had often walked through it and in his opinion there was nothing likely to make a man fall into it the way Hatto had. He added that Hatto, after this accident, went in the front of the house where Mary Ann used to sleep. Hatto called her name three or four times but nobody answered. He had then thrown something up at the window of her bedroom where Bunce noticed that that there was a light on. He did not go up at the front, he said, but had stood at the gates. He could, he added, see very well as it was a light night.

He had said to Hatto that he was going to bed again, but Hatto told him that he was not quite satisfied as he had heard a rumbling noise in the passage. Bunce told Hatto to try the passage door and Hatto replied that he had. He thought it was odd that Hatto had not mentioned that there might be some danger in the house. Bunce, by this time, must have been thoroughly fed up with Hatto's shenanigans for he went back to bed. Bunce was to say later that Hatto had said that there was someone about the place. Bunce commented that he thought he had heard steps in the courtyard.

Mary Slaymaker, a charwoman employed by Goodwin, was to say later that she took part in an experiment conducted in front of other witnesses which had included Goodwin, Ingleton, the builder of the farm, and Superintendent Perkins of the Eton Police, when she was to cry out, "Hatto! Hatto! Murder! Help!" The witnesses had lain on Hatto's bed as the experiment was carried out. They later said that they had distinctly heard her and they could have heard anyone going upstairs from the passage to the landing, though the kitchen and passage doors had been shut. Even Ingleton, who was suffering from a cold and slight deafness, could distinctly hear her calling out.

Superintendent Symington, who was described in the press as the '...active and intelligent Superintendent of Police for this district', had also attended the scene. He had found the trousers Hatto had worn on the night of Mary Ann's murder. He was encouraged to find that there were marks of blood on them. He was certain that they were human too, which was a great leap in the dark, as the test to distinguish between human and animal blood was many years off yet. He also found Hatto's jacket with blood on it, but it was pointed out to him that Hatto had assisted in removing the body of Mary Ann, so that he might have come in contact with her blood that way. Not discouraged, the 'active and intelligent Superintendent' discovered more blood on the bottom of Hatto's bed.

William Eggleton, who was employed as a servant, was called up by Goodwin on the night of the murder and went to the pump, mentioning something interesting to the investigating officers. Whilst in the bedroom with Hatto, he saw the groom lift up Mary Ann's body and take a bunch of keys out of one of her pockets. He also saw Hatto remove a handkerchief.

On the Thursday after the murder, Hatto told another of Goodwin's employees, Richard Binfield, a thresher, that he expected a parcel at Maidenhead Railway Station and that he should go for it and that he would take a horse. Hatto went on Goodwin's horse shortly before ten, and returned a little after eleven.

James Chamberlain was working as a porter at the railway station when Hatto had called asking for a parcel, but Chamberlain had told him that there was none for him. During the course of their conversation, Hatto told Chamberlain that he was the man the people suspected had murdered Mary Ann. Chamberlain thought that that was a rather strange thing to say as he had said nothing to him about the murder.

The Coroner's Inquest was opened the following day but was adjourned whilst the Police continued their enquiries into the case. The Windsor and Eton Express commented, '(Superintendent) Perkins and Superintendent Thomas of Slough have both been actively engaged in endeavouring to ascertain by whom this foul deed was committed'.

In the interim period, Goodwin discovered that certain items were missing from his dressing table. These included a pair of razors, a knife with several blades, an ivory tablet, a gold pencil case, a silver pencil case, a gold watch key, a gold pin, a gold ring and two small padlock keys.

As the Inquest resumed, and after Goodwin had given his evidence, Superintendent Symington announced that important evidence had been discovered '...against Hatto', and that he was now in custody on a Coroner's warrant.

At the conclusion of the Inquest, Hatto was committed to stand trial. His response was, "I can say nothing at all about the murder, except that I myself am innocent of the crime. I have nothing to say."

Symington later stated that as he conveyed Hatto to Aylesbury, there were a large number of people as they left Beaconsfield. "They were making a good deal of noise," the Superintendent said. "The prisoner grinned at them, grimaced and bowed to them." After a little while Hatto had said to the Superintendent, "The people think more of it than me. I don't fret, it's no use. What's done can't be helped. I suppose they'll do what they like with me." Later he had remarked to the Superintendent, "They say I took a handkerchief and keys from the deceased. I took the keys and gave them to Mr. Goodwin downstairs."

Hatto appeared at Buckinghamshire Assizes in March of 1854 where, after a two day trial, he was found guilty of the murder of Mary Ann Sturgeon and condemned to death.

The Judge, Lord Chief Justice Campbell, in passing sentence of death said that the prisoner was guilty of one of the most barbarous crimes in the annals of the country. As he passed sentence, his lordship appeared almost choked with emotion, according to a Court reporter. But the prisoner apparently heard both the verdict and the sentence with stolid indifference. In fact when told by the Lord Chief Justice to make his peace with God as there were no hopes of mercy for him in this world, Hatto raised his hand to his head and, making a respectful bow to the Judge, said, "Thank you, my Lord."

Whilst sojourning at the 'new' Aylesbury Gaol, Hatto made his confession in the presence of the Chaplain and the Governor. It was a long and rambling admission of guilt, in which he alleged that he had murdered Mary Ann because she had asked him to lend her some money. He had replied that had loaned money before and had not had it returned.

This remark, according to Hatto, apparently annoyed Mary Ann, who thereafter 'twitted' him about his conduct, and behaved generally in an ill-tempered manner towards him. He had also overheard Mary Ann and Bunce talking about him in a somewhat derogatory way, and he became very angry at not only hearing this conversation but because he felt that Mary Ann had been overworking him. Hatto had lost his temper and had murdered her. He had attacked her, first with a lard beater, and then he had kicked her, and finally had beaten her to death with the bloody poker found near her body. He had then set fire to her. His clothes, as might be expected, were in a bloody state and he had attempted to wash and hide them, but had decided to get rid of them by burying some of the items in the bank near the River Thames, which runs nearby. Other articles of clothing he had thrown into the river when he had 'borrowed' his master's horse and had ridden to Maidenhead Railway Station, making up the excuse that he was expecting a parcel.

Superintendent Symington and Mr. Charsley searched for the clothing and found a dirty, ragged shirt with bloodstains on it and some upper leathers, which appeared to have belonged to the murderer. No trace apparently was found of the stolen items.

Subsequently, after the conviction of Hatto and even after he had made a confession, three persons from Aylesbury journeyed to London to ask Lord Palmerston to commute the death sentence. Lord Palmerston reply to the deputation was, "... if the murderer escapes the death penalty of the law by the abrogation of capital punishment, crime will be more awful and revolting in this country. Those who meditate murder know that the gallows impends and are deterred. You cannot convince me that punishment of death has not this effect..."

An Aylesbury newspaper, the Bucks Herald, felt quite certain that the newspaper's readers would echo the Home Secretary's opinion, whilst it would have no objection to the execution taking place within the walls of the prison. The newspaper had no doubt whatever of the justice of the sentence.

This was carried out on 'the unfortunate wretch', who was executed on Friday, 24th March in front of the County Gaol at 8 a.m. before a large number of spectators. Hatto, according to the Under-Sheriff, conducted himself in a way '…entirely befitting his position, and that he died with Christian fortitude and resignation'.

It was, apparently, the first execution to have been carried out at the 'new' gaol, which had been built in Bierton Road. It was reported that, although a large number attended the hanging, there was no 'hooting or shouting, and when Hatto came forth, a breathless stillness pervaded the mass'.

The Windsor and Eton Express, which heretofore had praised the Police for their diligence, was now somewhat critical. 'They showed criminal negligence in permitting Hatto to roam at large and do as he pleased until he had disposed of almost all evidence of his guilt. But some excuse may be found for this remarkable apathy in the fact of the wretched man's good character'.

This was to be one of the last serious cases investigated under the 'old' system of law enforcement; the Parish Constable and the 'new', to Buckinghamshire, County Constabulary would be formed some three years later. It is speculative to consider if the new force would investigate serious crimes any better.

(1) As this was before the formation of the Buckinghamshire Constabulary, in 1857, the constables must have been Parish and Superintending Constables, and there seems to have been a number of them in attendance too.

(2) Maidenhead, which stands on the opposite side of the River Thames in Berkshire, had a small Borough Police under the terms of the Municipal Corporations Act of 1835. Although referred to in newspaper accounts as Chief Constable, he would more correctly be known as Superintendent or even Head Constable. The Home Office frowned on the use of the term 'Chief Constable' for small Borough Police forces, preferring that title for the head of the County Constabulary. Maidenhead Police was later amalgamated with the Berkshire Constabulary under the Local Government Act of 1888. See Indge.

MURDER OF A STAB-MONK (1)

CHALVEY - 1888

Edmund Higgins shivered as he stabled his employer's horse in the early evening of a cold December night in 1888. The rain stung his face and, as he and his employer, Charles Dance a coal dealer, left the latter's yard, both men turned up their collars in a forlorn attempt to keep the relentless rain from penetrating their sodden clothes still further. Higgins locked the gate to the yard and placed the key inside the window over the ledge. As he did so, Dance said, "I'll go and have a cup of tea and a wash and you come and give me a call after you've had a wash and a cup of tea and we'll go together." He was referring to the Christmas draw that was being held at The Garibaldi public house that night and, although both men were soaked through, they were rather looking forward to the night's entertainment, especially as the draw was for some beef, pork, fowls and four and a half gallons of beer. Something which, if they won, would make the season more festive. Both men parted, Higgins walking the fifty yards to his house in Chalvey, whilst Dance walked off in the direction of his.

Higgins did not delay, for half an hour later, at 7p.m., he was knocking on Dance's door. Mrs. Dance answered and informed Higgins that her husband had not yet been home. In view of the remarks made by Dance as they parted, Higgins gave her a quizzical look, then, shrugging his shoulders, walked the few yards to The Forester's Arms, which adjoined Dance's yard. Higgins opened the door and peered into the bar. Not seeing Dance, he enquired of the landlord, Mr. Lines, if the dealer had been in. Lines shook his head and replied that Dance had not been

Chalvey – late nineteenth century.

there. Higgins now made his way to The Garibaldi and asked the same question. Again he received a negative response, whereupon he decided to stop his rounds of the Chalvey public houses looking for his boss and to have a drink and wait for Dance to turn up.

At 8 p.m. Mrs. Dance had another caller, one William James, a gravel setter, who apparently also went under the surname of Atkins and who lived in High Street, Chalvey. He told her that a man wanted her husband by The Forester's Arms. Mrs. Dance told him, as she had told Higgins earlier, that her husband had not returned from his work. In fact the dealer did not return at all that evening and at 11 p.m. Mrs. Dance called at Higgins' house to find out if he had seen her husband. He had not, despite his vigil in The Garibaldi. Mrs. Dance returned home, assuming that her husband had gone to nearby Slough.

As he had still not come home by 5 o'clock the next morning, a by now frantic Mrs. Dance called again at Higgins' home and told him the worrying news. Higgins hurriedly dressed and went to the yard, where he found the stable door unlocked and the padlock hanging on a staple. Higgins entered the yard. His first concern was for the horse and accordingly he fed it. Then, going towards the chaff house, he noticed the body of Dance, lying across a wheelbarrow. Higgins went to it and held Dance's hand to see if there was any life but, as he later said, "…his hand felt as cold as day." Lighting a lantern, he held it so that he could see his master's body more clearly. He noticed that Dance's body bore marks of extreme violence and that he appeared quite dead.

Higgins dashed round to the local Constable's house and told P.C. Horne, who attended immediately. With the aid of his Bull's Eye lantern the constable inspected the terrible wounds that had been inflicted upon Dance. Sending Higgins for a doctor and further Police assistance from Slough, P.C. Horne remained at the scene.

He did not waste his time as he waited for reinforcements to arrive. The first thing he did was to search the clothes of the dead man. He found nothing in the left trouser pocket, but he thought that it had been pulled out by someone looking for something in a hurry. Going on to the other pocket, Horne discovered various items, including a draw ticket for The Garibaldi and a receipt for £6. 10/-. The constable now wandered over to the chaff house and, shining his lantern about, saw Dance's hat lying on the hay. Bearing in mind that Dance had reported to him quite recently the larceny of some chickens, Horne now went to the hen-house, but that was secure. He also noticed a truss of hay lying on the ground opposite the entrance to the shed, and remembered that the dealer had also told him that, whenever he had a new truss of hay, a local man named Roddy would invariably make his way into the yard and sleep there for a night or two. P.C. Horne, on one of his night patrols, had in fact turned Roddy out of Dance's yard when he had found him there himself. Horne examined the truss, but observed that it lay untouched and not as though anyone had sat on it.

Sergeant Hebbes now arrived, and P.C. Horne left to make a few enquiries of his own and to have a word with Mrs. Dance. On his return he conferred with his Sergeant, and as a result the two Policemen decided to go to the nearby gravel pit and speak to William James.

"You know poor old Charley Dance was murdered last night?" P.C.Horne said.

James stopped work; "I do," he replied.

"Did you see anything of him about anywhere?" asked the Constable.

James shook his head, "No."

"You went to his house last night," went on Horne. "What did you go there for? You are no friend of his, you know."

James paused for a second or two. "Well, I will tell you the truth, Horne. I was coming by Birdseye corner about half past seven, when I saw a gentleman standing there. He said to me, 'Young man, do you know where Mr. Dance is?' I said 'No. I will go and find him for you.' I saw Mrs. Dance and she said perhaps he was gone to The Garibaldi as he was in a draw. I came back and told him."

P.C. Horne glanced at James' feet. "Were those the shoes you were wearing last night, Roddy?" he asked, using the nickname that James went under.

"Yes," he replied. "That's all I've got."

Looking at James' coat, which lay on the ground nearby, Horne examined it and found a feather on a spot of blood sticking to the sleeve. Pointing this out to James, he asked where it had come from. Nonchalantly, James replied, "That came from the bed; I chucks my coat on it." Horne decided to seize the coat as possible evidence.

The two policemen left James and, going back to the scene of the murder, briefed Superintendent Dunham, the head of the Slough Police, who had, by now, arrived. Dr. Buce was also there in attendance and he made a careful examination of the body. Such had been the ferocity of the attack upon the dealer that the force of the blows had driven the dealer's palate into his throat. The doctor also discovered some wounds which, he conjectured, had been caused by a garden fork.

Dunham listened carefully to what his officers had to say and decided that he would pay a visit to James' landlady, Mrs. Moody. She told the Superintendent that her lodger had arrived home at about 5.50 p.m. on the Friday evening, had his tea and went out. He had returned about 7.50 p.m. when he had 'slushed' his face with water in the outhouse, emptying the pail of water down the drain between the houses. James had then left his lodgings within ten minutes, telling Mrs. Moody that he was going to the slate club at The White Hart public house. He had returned just after 10 p.m., when he mentioned that he had seen a woman known locally as 'Whoops, my darling', a female of doubtful virtue. He had then paid Mrs. Moody 1/6d. for rent, though in fact he owed her a total of 6/6d. Mrs. Moody also disclosed that she had asked James every night of the previous week and again on the Friday morning for the money outstanding, but James had insisted that he did not have a halfpenny.

To Superintendent Dunham this was very interesting news and he was determined to interview James himself. Accordingly, with Horne and Hebbes, he now went to the gravel pit where he saw James at work and put a few pertinent questions to him. "What time did you return to your lodgings from your work last night?" he asked.

"Half past five and I did not go out again until eight. I then went to Glass's beerhouse, (The Flags in Chalvey), and remained there until ten when I came home and bought a pint of beer in a bottle. I hotted it, drank it and went to bed."

"Did you meet anybody on your road to Glass's?" enquired the Superintendent.

"Yes," answered James. "I saw a gentleman standing by Lines and he asked me if I had seen Mr. Dance. I said, 'No, perhaps he's around home, I'll go and see.'" James repeated to the Superintendent what he had previously told his two subordinates, that he had called on Mrs. Dance and been told that her husband was not at home. She said that she thought her husband had gone round to The Garibaldi as he was in a draw there. James had returned to the gentleman and informed him that Dance was not at home. He had then volunteered to call at The Forester's Arms to see if the coal dealer was in there. Within a few

The Flags public house, Chalvey

minutes he had returned to say that Dance was not there either.

Dunham regarded the gravel setter with steely eyes. "You tell a very different story from what your landlady does. Will you come with us and see her?"

As James prepared to accompany the Police officers to his lodgings, Dunham continued, "She says you paid her eighteen pence last night."

"So I did," replied James. "It was money as Seymour (James' employer) paid me the night before." He explained that Seymour had paid him money, some of which he had changed in The Flags the night of the murder and he had given Mrs. Moody 1/6d. on his return.

The little party left the gravel pit and walked to James' lodgings. Mrs. Moody was not there but James' mother was. P.C. Horne asked where her son had been the previous night. "Why, he came to the laundry window three times," she replied. Mrs. James worked at the local wash-house.

"Let's start at number one," the Constable said. "What time was that?"

"Eight o'clock," she replied.

"Now for number two," requested Horne.

34

"The third time he came was between nine and ten," was the response.

Horne was not satisfied with her answer and pressed her on the point. "I have not done number two yet, let's have that."

Mrs. James hesitated, "I don't know," she mumbled. The three Policemen looked knowingly at each other.

It was at this juncture that Mrs. Moody returned and Dunham observed James winking at her as though trying to tell her something. This action was not lost on the other Police Officers either. Dunham told James that he must attend the Inquest that would be opened that day at The Cape of Good Hope, (yet another Chalvey public house).

At the Inquest James was called and he repeated the story he had told the Superintendent of finishing work and arriving at his lodgings just after 5 p.m. and not leaving before 8 o'clock. He had gone, first of all, to the laundry where his mother worked and had joked with her through a window. He had then walked to Birdseye corner, Chalvey, where he had met a 'gentleman', who had asked him where Dance was. James gave a description of this man and also stated that he had seen him before in the district.

Mrs. Moody said that James had come home, had his tea and gone out, returning about 8 p.m. He had sluiced his face in a pail of water in the outhouse and then thrown the water down the drain between the backs of the houses. James had then told Mrs. Moody that he was going to The White Hart, where he was in the slate club, to get some money. He left her lodgings again and returned shortly after 10 o'clock, when he had given her 1/6d. Mrs. Moody was adamant that James had left her house for the first time before 6 p.m. and, when questioned by Superintendent Dunham, told the Inquest that she had been in the house between 6 p.m. and 8 p.m. and James had not been in the house during those times.

As the coroner adjourned the Inquest, Superintendent Dunham caused a sensation by arresting James and taking him to Slough Police Station. In the meantime, he instructed his men to search the gravel pits, where the prisoner worked, in an effort to find either the murdered man's money, the weapon or any other clues that might assist in the

Slough High Street – showing the Police Station where the suspect was taken. (Twentieth century view)

investigation.

James was lodged in the cells over Christmas and his next public appearance was at the Petty Sessions on 26th December charged with murder. He was described by one reporter as aged 23 years, 5'8", fair complexion with dark brown hair and he had '...sinister eyes and a querulous mouth, but beyond this there is nothing unpleasant in his countenance'. He was said to be '...looking rather pale but otherwise there is nothing to indicate that he felt the seriousness of his position and paid great attention to the evidence that was given'.

Mrs. Moody was able to give more details of the strange goings on of her former lodger that Friday night. James, she said, had called back about 8 p.m. when he had taken off his boots, which he placed on the fire, and he had then removed his jacket. He asked Mrs. Moody for a rag to dry his feet, as he wore no socks. As he did so, Mrs. Moody stared at the smouldering boots in the fire. James then went to the wash-house, filled a pail with water and washed himself, afterwards throwing the water down the brick channel used by Mrs. Moody's house and her neighbour's. After drying himself on the towel hanging on the back door, James left the house. Mrs. Moody noticed some dark stains on the towel that James had used. Her lodger had returned with a pint of beer in a pickle bottle which he warmed, added some ginger to and drank whilst he sat talking to Mr. Moody. James had then paid her some of the rent that he owed her. When she had asked for more, he put her off by saying that he would pay her in the morning. James had then gone to bed about 11.30 p.m.

At 6.30 a.m. the following morning, she continued, her husband had gone to waken James. He was in a deep sleep and appeared to be having a nightmare, for he called out, "Charley! Charley! Charley!" before Mr. Moody could wake him up. James rose, dressed and had then left the house, but had returned about five minutes later, saying, "Poor old Dance is dead in his yard; died suddenly."

After he had told the Moodys this astonishing piece of news, he left once more. A little later that morning Mrs. Moody was talking to one of her neighbours, who had pointed out to her some 'lumps' of blood in the drain where James had emptied the pail of water the night before after washing himself. Mrs. Moody had also seen some drops of blood leading from the wash-house to the back door. Without any more ado the two women had set to and swept the blood away.

Mrs. Moody said that she was then visited by Mrs. James, her lodger's mother, who lived nearby, and they were discussing the death of Charles Dance when James called in again. Mrs. James asked her son if Dance had died suddenly or had been murdered, but all that James could mutter was, "They've got my jacket," meaning the Police. As Mrs. Moody, her lodger and his mother sat down to have breakfast, Mrs. Moody asked James if it was correct that the Police had indeed taken his jacket. James looked her straight in the eye and made the astonishing request, "If they come to know whether I was out at the time, say I was out till after eight."

After eating his breakfast, Mrs. Moody added, James once more left his lodgings, only to return around mid-day. This time he was accompanied by Superintendent Dunham and, whilst there, James had continually winked at her, as if he was trying to impart something. However, this was lost on Mrs. Moody.

Another thing that Mrs. Moody mentioned was that, when James had left her house just before 6 p.m., he had been wearing a belt around his waist, yet when he came in at 8 p.m. James told her that he had lost it. She recalled him saying, "I would not have lost it for 5/-." He asked her if there was anything she could lend him to support his trousers. Mrs. Moody had fetched an old woollen necktie that belonged to her husband, which James had tied around his middle.

Referring to the boots that James had put on the fire, Mrs. Moody imparted to the court that they were an old pair of light lace-up boots which she had never seen before that night.

James cross-examined her, asking if she had not washed any giblets or meat in the drain on Friday evening. This Mrs. Moody emphatically denied. When he asked her about the jacket that he had worn on the fatal evening, Mrs. Moody answered that the jacket he now had on in the Courtroom was not the only one he had been wearing, for he had also worn the one that the Police had seized. James also maintained that he had been at her lodgings between 6 p.m. and 8 p.m. but Mrs. Moody would not be shaken on this matter either and reiterated that James had not been there during those times. A reporter for a local newspaper noted that James seemed very anxious to shake Mrs. Moody's evidence on this particular matter, almost trying to put the answers he wanted into her mouth. As the reporter added, 'There is no actual proof that the murder was committed between 6 p.m. and 8 p.m. and therefore, unless the prisoner is acting upon some knowledge possessed by himself alone, his anxiety to show that he was at home during these hours is somewhat inexplicable'.

At this stage the court was adjourned and, as the prisoner was led off by his Police escort, he remarked, "I wish you a happy New Year when it comes."

When the Inquest was resumed, William Seymour, who employed James, was called before the Coroner. He said that he gave James a half a crown, 2/6d, a day and a pint of beer and paid him on Saturdays. On 15th December Seymour had handed over to James the sum of 3/6d. The next day he let James have 1/6d. as a sub for the following week. Thereafter he gave him 2d. a night for the next five nights.

Thomas Austin of Chalvey was the next to give evidence. He said that he had met James at Birdseye corner at 7.30 p.m. on the night of the murder. James approached him and asked if he could lend him 2d., as he had no money and wanted a pint of beer. He added that he would have some money the next night, when he would repay him. Austin gave him the 2d., and walked off. As he did so he heard someone clamber over a fence in the vicinity of Dance's yard, but hearing no further sounds had carried on towards Slough.

Alfred Glass, the landlord of The Flags beerhouse, said he noticed James come into his place a little after 8 o'clock that night and have a pint of beer for which he paid 2d. About an hour later he called for a pot of beer and, throwing down a 2/- piece, said, "Take it out of that."

Mrs. Dance, the widow, was called and shown a bag which had been seized from Mrs. Moody's grate by the Police and which had been placed there by James. She said that it was similar to the pouch used by her husband for his money.

Mr. Bray, the clerk to a coal merchant in Chalvey, said that Dance had called on him on 21st December and had taken money from a bag similar to the one he was now shown. He thought that Dance's bag was lighter and not as worn as that shown at the inquest.

Thomas Lines of The Forester's Arms said that Dance's money bag was darker and longer than the one he now looked at.

James Catherwood of The White Hart firmly stated that James was no longer in the slate club. He had been once but had become a defaulter and had therefore forfeited all claims. He added that James had not been in his public house on the fatal Friday night, which was not altogether surprising as he owed money to Catherwood. Neither had that doyenne

The Forester's Arms public house, Chalvey

of Chalvey night life, 'Whoops, my darling', visited his pub that night.

The next witness, Joseph Swain, had a very interesting story to tell. He had left his house in Chalvey between twenty past and half past seven on the Friday night. He was walking in the direction of the High Street and as he crossed the road he saw a tall man get over the fence of Dance's yard. He had thought no more about it until the next morning, when he heard of the murder of the coal dealer. Swain said that the man had had a coat on just like the one the Police had produced in evidence. It was raining hard at the time of this incident and he saw the man get over and jump down. When asked how he was so sure that the coat now in Court was similar to the one he had seen that dark, dismal Friday night, he replied that he had noticed it by the lamplight near the Forester's Arms.

Once more the Inquest was adjourned, but only a few days later the witnesses reassembled for the hearing at the Petty Sessions. (It seems curious now that two courts were running at the same time, going over the same evidence. Each time, however, the witnesses seemed to add a little more to the build up of the case against the prisoner, James.)

Mrs. Moody, for example, when she was telling the Court about her lodger, added that he had pushed some 'dirty stuff' into the boots which were placed on the fire and which looked similar to the bag now before the Magistrates. Again, when describing her lodger's behaviour at the breakfast table, she remarked to him, "You don't know anything about the murder, do you?" He had replied, "Only a man met me in the passage when I went out at 8 o'clock."

Mrs. Moody had shrugged her shoulders. "I don't want the bother of it," she had said, adding, "And I hope they won't come here," referring to the Police.

James had said, "You needn't trouble. Say I was not out until after 8 o'clock." James had continued that the man he had met in the passage had asked him where Dance had lived. "Should you know the man again?" enquired Mrs. Moody.

"No," replied James.

"If you do it will clear you," she had pointed out.

"I went to Dance's house but did not take the man with me," James answered.

Dr. Buce, who had conducted the post-mortem on Dance, revealed the horrific injuries that the coal dealer had suffered. His head had been terribly battered and there was a mark around his neck as though he had been dragged by something around it to the spot where he had been discovered by Higgins on the Saturday morning.

A solicitor was now acting for James and he enquired about an injury that his client had sustained. Dr. Buce explained that when he had examined James he had found that he had a wound on his right wrist that would have affected the power of his hand. The flexure of his muscles had been divided, he went on, and this would have affected the grasp of his hand and, to a lesser extent, the striking power of his arm. However, Dr. Buce remarked, the weakening of the right arm would have led to the strengthening of his left.

Questioned about the injuries to Dance, the doctor went on to say that he thought that some of the blows on the back of the head might have been given from behind, and the wound to the mouth might have been caused by a kick. If that were so it must have been by a heavy boot. He had to admit, under cross-examination, that it could not have been done by a light boot.

The Public Analyst, Mr. W.W. Fisher, now stepped into the box. He had, he stated, received from P.C.Horne a sack containing a hat, a coat, a pair of trousers and a towel, and was asked to examine these articles for bloodstains. He had not found any upon either the sack or the hat, but he had discovered a spot of blood upon the right sleeve of the coat with a small feather stuck to it. He had also found some bloodstains on the trousers. He had also looked carefully at the towel. There were, he explained, no distinct signs of blood, although there were some pinkish looking stains and some brownish stains. He had cut out some pieces from the towel and washed the stains with water, but had not obtained any evidence of blood.

Mr. Fisher was closely questioned about the bloodstains found on the clothing of the prisoner and asserted that they could have been washed or may have been saturated with rain. He was unable to say whether they were human bloodstains.

James' solicitor wanted to know more about the feather and the blood to which it had been attached. Mr. Fisher said that he had spent two or three days examining the blood, but could not determine whether it belonged to a fowl or a mammal. He added that the feather had been preserved by him and was in his possession under lock and key. James' solicitor looked at the witness. "My client's life may depend upon that feather," he remarked.

Austin was also cross-examined and declared that he had been about 25 yards from the fence when he had heard the noise of someone clambering over, but could not say if it was the prisoner, James. He did say, however, that when James had asked him for the loan of the money he seemed very nervous and was stuttering a great deal before he got the words out.

Dr. Buce added to the evidence he had given before that the mark on Dance's neck could have been made by a cord or a belt.

The Police now produced another piece of evidence that had been found in Mrs. Moody's grate, a belt buckle which, they would have the Court believe, had been discarded by James on one of his return trips to his lodgings on the night of the murder.

The Inquest jury, after having been addressed by the Coroner, had little hesitation in finding a verdict of murder against James and he was duly committed to the Buckinghamshire Assizes.

He appeared before Sir James Fitzjames Stephen in February. To the Slough Observer reporter, the prisoner looked to be '...in good health and spirits and seemed either callous to the serious position he now found himself in or supremely confident of being acquitted'. Looking around, the journalist pictured the scene for his readers. 'The Court was crowded, those present including many ladies who could not but feel that the sight of a human creature being tried for his life was one admirably suited to their sex'.

The case was opened for the Prosecution, and the witnesses who had given evidence at the Slough Petty Sessions and the Coroner's Inquest were called once again and put through their paces.

Mr. Attenborough, for the defence, asked the jury to believe that the murderer, far from being the man now in the dock, was probably a tramp who had taken the weapon away with him after committing the deed, which was the reason why it had not been found, despite an intensive Police search for it. He said that his client had, in actual fact, been out fowl stealing on Friday, 21st December, and the amount of money he had during the course of the evening had been obtained by the sale of some of the proceeds of his extra-curricular activities. He called upon Mrs. Ann Stanley of Chalvey, who recollected seeing James between 7.30 p.m. and 8 p.m. the night that Dance had been killed. He had knocked on her back door and, when her husband had answered, he had invited James in. James had asked the Stanleys if they would like two fowls and when they replied that they would, had offered them two at 2/6d. Mr. Stanley bargained with his caller, saying that he could only afford 2/- and a pint of beer, to which James had agreed. He had then left their house, only to return about ten minutes later with the fowls.

Not wishing to go out on such a night as it was to fetch a pint of beer, Mr. Stanley and James had settled on the sum of 2/2d., which Mrs. Stanley had given him; a two shilling piece and two pennies. James had then left their house, saying he would go and have a drink, and wished the Stanleys the compliments of the season.

Of course, Mrs. Stanley was rigorously cross-examined. She responded that, although she had known the prisoner for some time, she was no particular friend of his. She had not realised the significance of the transaction that had taken place that December night until later, when she had been approached by James' solicitor. She had to agree with the Prosecution counsel that she had not volunteered this information to the Police. She had no idea that the transaction was anything but above board. If she had she would not, she affirmed, have had anything to do with it.

After a long summing up by the Judge, the jury retired to consider their verdict. As the moment of decision arrived, the prisoner was seen by the Slough Observer reporter to have sobered down and to have become somewhat anxious. The jury deliberated for an hour and then returned. In answer to the question put to them by the Clerk, the foreman announced that they considered James was 'Not Guilty' of the murder!

James stepped as quickly as he could from the dock and returned to Slough, where he was greeted by several people who shook hands with him. "They took a rope to hang me with," he joked with his new found friends, "but they have had to bring it back again." Feeling quite dry after his ordeal, he repaired to a local public house and slaked his thirst.

The mystery of who killed Charles Dance was never solved. The Slough Observer urged the Police to find the man who had enquired of James the whereabouts of the coal dealer but, despite adding that no doubt James would be anxious to assist the authorities, the man was never found.

So the mystery remains. Did James murder Charles Dance? Did he invent the story of being accosted by the man at Birdseye corner? According to him, he certainly went out of his way to 'oblige' the unknown gentleman by calling on Mrs. Dance and by visiting The Forester's Arms, when he could have easily directed him to the Dances' house, which was only a few yards away. After all, on his own admission he received no recompense for his trouble in so doing. Then there were the nods and winks he gave Mrs. Moody about not divulging to the Police that he had gone out of her house before 8 p.m., when he had already admitted to the Police that he been to call on Mrs. Dance at 7.30 p.m. Or was he indeed up to his old tricks as the late Charles Dance and P.C. Horne had no doubt suspected him, of stealing fowls from the coal dealer's yard? Why had Dance returned to his yard instead of going the few yards to his home? Had he heard someone about in the yard? Or was he just being over cautious? Whatever the reason, he met a sudden and very violent death there.

For Superintendent Dunham, one of the original Police Officers to have been appointed on the formation of the Buckinghamshire Constabulary in 1857, the case must have been another disappointment. Since his success in solving the Denham murders of 1870 (2), all other murder cases had ended in acquittals. There had been the Reville case of 1881, when he had arrested one of the employees for the murder of Mrs. Reville (3), and the slaying of Francis Carter in 1882, when the man he had arrested had not even been committed to the Assizes but had been discharged by the Magistrates (4). Now there was this case. He had been so sure that he had the right man, but there was little direct evidence to convict James, and forensic evidence was still an obscure science. Then, when the defence had sprung upon them witnesses from right under the Police noses, who stated that James had sold them some fowls on the night of the murder, and who, it would appear, had been believed by the jury, it must have come as a bitter blow to him and all the Police officers engaged in the case.

Perhaps all that James was guilty of was a little stealing now and then to help pay for his beer and his rent, and it was quite coincidental that the same night that he was out and about stealing and selling chickens, Charles Dance was murdered. No one will ever know for certain.

One more curious matter was reported in the Slough Observer a couple of months after the trial, when an item appeared in that newspaper that a coal hammer had been found in Seymour's gravel pits which had at some time been placed in a fire. Was this, the newspaper queried, the murder weapon the Police had searched for in vain in December the previous year? It was just such a weapon that would have caused many of the wounds inflicted on Dance, it argued. The matter was laid quietly to rest.

(1) For many years the inhabitants of Chalvey were known as 'Stabmonks'. Maxwell Fraser, in her book, The History of Slough, published in 1973, says that in the mid to late nineteenth century a child was bitten by a monkey kept by an Italian organ grinder. When the child reported the incident to his father, he rushed out and stabbed the offending monkey to death. A collection was made for the organ grinder and a funeral was held for the late, lamented monkey and there was enough left over for a 'wake'. It was so successful that it was decided to celebrate the occasion by holding a wake every year on the anniversary of the incident.

(2) See 'Murder in Buckinghamshire' by the author.

(3) Ibid.

(4) See 'Buckinghamshire Murders' by the author.

"YOU'LL MARRY HER OVER MY DEAD BODY!"

HAVERSHAM - 1938

The small village of Haversham lies just a short distance from Wolverton along the main railway line from London to Glasgow. A more tranquil place one could hardly imagine. Yet, early in the 11th century Saxons and Danes had fought bloody skirmishes in the locality as each side wantonly plundered, burnt and killed as they wandered over the land. In 1010, the Norsemen exacted a bloody price for earlier incursions by the Saxons into what they saw as their portion of England. For three months they raided Oxfordshire and Buckinghamshire, attacking Buckingham itself and Newport Pagnell as they roamed along the River Ouse. A few years later, after the Norman Conquest had taken place, Haversham snuggled down for centuries of relative peace.

The next biggest upheaval would come with the construction of the London to Birmingham Railway in the nineteenth century with its attendant hordes of 'navvies' passing through the village, no doubt terrifying the local population with their raucous and drunken ways, until they passed on to another part of the country.

Years went by and Haversham slumbered on. The Great War came and took its toll of men fighting for King and Country, as it did of every village, town and city throughout the land, and then peace returned once more.

North west Buckinghamshire in the 1930s, despite having numerous brick works in the area, the massive L.M.S Railway Carriage Works and McQuordale's paper works, both at Wolverton, was still largely rural and the many farms dotted about the countryside bore testimony to this.

47

The main towns in the area were Bletchley, Stony Stratford, Wolverton and Newport Pagnell. Agriculture had been going through lean times since the end of The Great War. It would eventually prosper during the years of the Second World War and afterwards.

In the late 1930s, people were in general slightly better off than they had been during the depths of the Great Depression a few years before, and advertisements in the local papers, in February of 1938, generally reflected this. One could, for instance, buy an Austin Big Seven Economy saloon car for £145 or a Flying Standard nine horse power saloon for £152.10s (£152.50p).

For those who could not afford a car, and they were in the majority, the answer was public transport. The London Midland and Scottish Railway were offering return fares from Wolverton to London at 4/2d (21p).

On turning the pages of the local newspaper, the Wolverton Express, there was an announcement for the grand opening of the Money Savings Stores in High Street, Stony Stratford. They were making a special offer for two days only of 1 lb. of sugar, free with every purchase of 2/6d (15p) worth of gifts. Soups were priced at 5 1/2d (2 1/2p), jam at 7 1/2d per jar (3p), whilst three large tins of plums could be bought for 1/- (5p). At the Co-Op a bar of CWS New Sheaf Olive Oil Soap cost 5d (2p) and a packet of Alono Washing Powder was 3d (well under 2p), or you could purchase them both for 5 1/2d (approx. 2 1/2p).

At Fosters a suit could be made to measure from 45 shillings (£2.25p) and a 'smart raincoat' varied between 21 shillings (£1. 5p) and 35 shillings (£1.75p).

The Co-Op was also offering a light Roadster pedal cycle for £5.10/- (£5.50p) and prams from £3.12/6d (£3.62 1/2p). H.H. Lampitt of Stratford Road, Wolverton, advertised a Murphy's wireless set for £8.5/- (£8.25p) and Stanifords, the wine and spirits "Butlers" of Wolverton, had a sale of rich Australian red and white wine at 2/6d (12 1/2p) per bottle.

There was, in the first week of February 1938, plenty of entertainment, mainly of the cinematic variety, on offer. At the New Empire at Wolverton,

Wolverton in the 1930s.

Akim Tamiroff was starring in 'The Great Gambini'. The film 'Parnell' with Clarke Gable and Myrna Loy was at the Palace, Wolverton, from the 3rd February whilst at the Scala, Stony Stratford, Arthur Lucan and Kitty McShane were in 'Old Mother Riley'. The Electra Cinema, at Newport Pagnell, boasted Clarke Gable in another of his many films 'Saratoga', this time his co-star being Jean Harlow. At the New Empire the Chums Meeting on Saturday advertised a showing of the Range Riders and seats were priced at 6d and 9d (2 1/2p and approx. 4p).

If, however, one wished to visit a theatre, Northampton was not too far away and there one could be entertained at the Repertory Theatre by the Leon Gordon play 'White Cargo', whilst at the New Theatre Bebe Daniels and Ben Lyon were appearing in variety.

Wolverton in the 1930s.

The citizens of Wolverton, Stony Stratford, Newport Pagnell and the villages between them could thus have enjoyed all these distractions if they wished to. They were unaware of the tragedy that was about to be played out in their midst.

Fields Farm, Haversham, is within a few yards of the L.M.S. railway line and was owned by Thomas Harry Robinson, who had bought it some ten years before. In February 1938, Thomas was convalescing at a hospital in Wimbledon, leaving the actual management of the farm and its 147 acres to his wife Lizzie Tryphena age 63 years and their son John Thomas Paul Robinson 27 years, an only child. The Robinsons were well known in the locality, Thomas having worked at the family building firm for several years before purchasing the farm, whilst John was quite

50

a sporty fellow, being a member of Wolverton Town Cricket Club and captain of the Haversham village team. He also enjoyed badminton and table tennis, and as both mother and son were devoted to each other John would often convey his mother to cricket matches. Life appeared to be drifting on quite pleasantly but there was a very dark cloud hanging over the family.

In the early morning of Friday, 4th February the employees who worked at Fields Farm sensed nothing wrong as they went about their early morning labours. Having finished these and gone for their breakfasts, they returned to the farm to complete their other work, and were somewhat surprised to see the blinds of the farmhouse still drawn. Especially as John Robinson was usually working around the farm before breakfast himself. One of the workers, Frank Chown, went to the house and looked in and must have wished that he had not, for there, lying on the floor, was the bloody corpse of John Robinson.

The Police were contacted and Sergeant Gee of Wolverton was the first Policeman to attend the scene, and as he entered the farmhouse he encountered the body of John, lying in the sitting room with terrible head wounds and a shotgun beside him. John's pet Aberdeen terrier was pathetically guarding his master's body and, as can be imagined under the circumstances, was in a frantic state. Sergeant Gee walked stealthily through the house wondering what else he would find, as he was aware that Mrs. Robinson was still unaccounted for. As he reached her bedroom he realised that she would never be seen busy about the farm again, for there, lying face down with horrific head wounds, lay her lifeless body.

Sergeant Gee, realising that this was a very serious matter indeed, contacted his superior officers. In due course, Superintendent Ernest Callaway of Bletchley attended, accompanied by Inspector Browning from Newport Pagnell. The Superintendent took charge of the investigation, and shortly afterwards Dr. Fildes from Wolverton also drove up to the farm. He had initially to confirm that both persons were dead, a task which seemed obvious to everyone who saw the two bodies but something that was required by law. Then, when the bodies had been removed, the doctor could conduct a full post-mortem examination, which hopefully would assist the Police in determining the sequence of events leading up to the deaths.

A number of Constables were placed around the farm to protect the scene from unwarranted intrusion. A necessary precaution as it transpired, for when the news leaked out hundreds of people came to the farmhouse over the weekend out of morbid curiosity.

An Inquest was opened on the Monday following the deaths. The Coroner, Mr R.D. Walton, informed everyone that he would hear evidence of formal identification and cause of death in order that the bodies could be released for the funerals. Mr. George Robinson then said that he had seen the bodies of his sister-in-law and nephew, whilst Dr. Fildes gave a short resume of the deceaseds' injuries. In relation to Mrs. Robinson he had found a depressed fracture of the skull which had probably been caused by a blunt instrument and which might have caused her death. In addition there was a gunshot wound through the left ear which went in a slanting direction through the head and had blown out the right side of her face. If the first wound had not caused her death, he emphasised, then the second would certainly have done so.

The doctor now turned to the injuries to John Robinson. The cause of death was due to a gunshot wound travelling through the right eye, blowing out the upper left part of the skull and blowing out the brain too.

Mr. Walton then adjourned the Inquest to the evening of Saturday, 12th February to enable the Police to carry out their enquiries and to ascertain why such a calamity should have befallen the family. What they discovered, and the reason behind the shootings, would be revealed at the resumption of the hearing. Then, it was hoped, the full reason for the tragic events at Fields Farm would be revealed.

On the 12th February the inquest was resumed and a jury was sworn in. Dr. Fildes was recalled and he described in greater detail the wounds that he had found at the post –mortem. The gunshot wound to Mrs. Robinson, he said, was so close to the head that it had blown a clear hole right through of about ¾ inch to an inch in diameter. There was blackening and scorching to the wound, he added, and the entry was so small it showed that the gun must have been right up against the ear when it had been fired. If it had been only two to three inches away from the head the entrance wound would have been larger. He was of the opinion that Mrs. Robinson must have been on the floor when the gun had been discharged and that she must have been unconscious at the time, for in addition there was a serious wound to the top of her head which had caused a depressed fracture of the skull. Both wounds, he admitted, would have caused death. In fact, Mrs. Robinson would have been dying when she was shot. He had also found another minor wound on the back of the neck. He was quite definite that the wounds were not self-inflicted.

Dr. Fildes now referred to his notes on the post-mortem he had carried out on the body of John Robinson which had been discovered in the sitting room of the house. He had been lying on his back and a gunshot wound had been seen close to his right eye, with scorching and blackening surrounding the entrance. The wound was, the doctor added, compatible with self-infliction.

When asked by Mr. Walton how long he thought the Robinsons had been dead, Dr. Fildes estimated between twelve to twenty hours before he had first seen them shortly after 10 o'clock on the morning of February 4th.

In answer to a question from the foreman of the jury, the doctor replied that it appeared that a struggle had taken place between the deceased persons in the sitting room of the house.

Mr. W.S.Bull, solicitor acting on behalf of the Robinson family, then stood up. "I am going to produce evidence that Mr. and Mrs. Harry Robinson were first cousins," he said," and that Mr. John Robinson was a child of the marriage of first cousins. I want to ask you whether the child of first cousins could be said to be more likely to develop an unbalanced mind than a child by parents unrelated?"

"I think the answer is yes," was Dr. Fildes' response.

Next to give evidence was Superintendent Callaway and he recounted how he had been called out to Fields Farm and had seen the bodies. He had observed the shotgun by the corpse of John Robinson in the sitting room. He had also noticed an Aladdin lamp on a table in the same room. The lamp was dry, the Superintendent went on, the oil having presumably burnt out during the course of the night of February 3rd to 4th. Also on the table were writing materials and an unfinished letter written by Mrs. Robinson. Superintendent Callaway had, as a matter of course, read the unfinished missive which was in reply to one that he had also found at the scene, hastily adding that they were quite unrelated to the events that had taken place that night. However, the Police officer produced both letters in case the Coroner or the jury wished to inspect them. As he handed them over to Mr. Walton, Superintendent Callaway remarked that the letter written by Mrs. Robinson bore a smudge, as if the writer had got up in a hurry and had smeared it with her hand.

The Coroner looked at the letters and, indicating some stains that he found, enquired of the senior Police Officer, "These marks are blood splashes?"

"Yes sir," the Superintendent replied firmly, before continuing with his evidence. Also on the table were socks, which were apparently being darned, a couple of newspapers and a woman's handbag. Lying on the hearthrug was a pair of spectacles. A chair with a cushion was overturned and a bricklayer's hammer lay close to the cushion. When he had looked at the hammer he had seen a hair attached to it, and he had arranged to have the hammer examined at the Metropolitan Police Laboratory, but they had found that it was not a human hair. Neither, curiously, had they found any bloodstains on it.

The Superintendent related how he had moved along the hall where he had found a discharged shotgun cartridge. He had also observed spots of blood along the wall as well. When he had reached the front bedroom he had seen the body of Mrs. Robinson lying face down on the floor. The injuries were exactly as Dr. Fildes had previously described.

Charles Greenhill of Stony Stratford now stepped up to give evidence. He had known the Robinson family since 1923, he informed the Inquest, and six years ago he had sold a gun to John. He had spent a good deal of time with him and had on occasions gone out shooting with him.

Prompted by the Coroner, Mr. Greenhill recalled an incident that had occurred some years before when he and John had gone out shooting, taking a dog with them. "The dog put a rabbit out of a hedge and followed it. Robinson called the dog but it did not come back for some time. When it did return Robinson hit it with a stick," the witness recounted. He had struck it rather a lot in Greenhill's opinion and he had protested, "If you insist on hitting the dog I shall hit you." Robinson had dropped the stick, picked up his gun and Greenhill had become fearful that his companion was about to shoot him. Greenhill had shouted at him and Robinson had pulled himself together and had fallen in with his friend's suggestion that they had better return home.

"That indicated to you that he had a very violent temper?" queried the Coroner.

"Yes!" emphatically replied the witness. He readily admitted to being frightened at this outburst and that to him, John appeared unbalanced.

Mr. Walton now asked Greenhill about John Robinson's relationship with a Stony Stratford woman, Kathy Peirce (1), "...he told me in the early days that he did not intend to get married to her. His mother was very much against it but it sort of developed later on and his mother used to talk to me about it." Greenhill added that in fact both John's parents were against the relationship.

Later John had told Greenhill that he had married Kathy, and the two men had pondered over who should tell John's mother. John had thought this over and had said that he would tell her himself. Greenhill had not thought that it was a wise decision, as Mrs. Robinson was known to have a violent temper.

The Coroner enquired of the witness if that had meant bad blood between mother and son. "Only at times when it cropped up. At other times they thought the world of each other," Greenhill replied.

Superintendent Callaway sought clarification on this point by asking, "When the matter of this lady cropped up between them, they were in a temper with each other?"

"Sometimes," Greenhill replied. "It depended on how much it was brought up."

This mention of a lady's name connected to John Robinson had by now taken the interest of all those who attended the Inquest, and the next witness was able to throw more light onto the matter.

Walter Ansell, a builder's manager who worked daily with John, revealed how, one Friday, John had confided to him that he had obtained a special licence and intended to get married. "I told him, 'you are a long time married you know'."

John had replied that he had not told his parents. "It would not matter if I lived to be fifty or sixty, they would never consent to my marriage."

Ansell had been present at John and Kathy's wedding on 3rd January of that year but since then no reference had been made to the marriage at all. He had last seen John on 3rd February as he left work at the farm, and he thought that there was nothing peculiar about John then.

A local postman revealed that he had called later that evening and John Robinson had come out of the farmhouse to the post van and collected a letter. As the two men chatted, the postman could see Mrs. Robinson standing by a table in the kitchen. John had then returned to the farmhouse and the postman had driven away up the long drive to the road. He would appear to have been the last person to have seen mother and son alive.

There was a stirring in the Court as the next witness was called. "Mrs. Robinson!" All eyes turned to see a young woman dressed in mourning as she made her way slowly to the witness box. She gave her name and stated that she was the widow of John Robinson. Everyone strained forward to hear what she had to say, for she spoke in hushed tones.

She agreed with the Coroner that her late husband's parents had been strongly opposed to the marriage, and that it had been Mrs. Robinson's objections to it that had caused her husband to keep it a secret from his mother.

Mr. Walton asked her if it was correct that if her husband's mother would not have accepted Kathy and the marriage, John would have got a job and supported her on his own account. "That is so," she answered softly.

The Coroner attempted to clarify the situation by saying that it was suggested that there was nothing in the least against Kathy except the thought that, as so many mothers-in-law do, perhaps she was not in such a good social position as her son. (The new Mrs. Robinson was employed in the Binding Department at McQuordales.)

Kathy quietly replied, "That was all there was in it sir." She added that her husband had definitely not informed his mother.

Kathy told the Inquest that she had not seen her husband on the night of February 3rd.

Mrs. Robinson was the last of the witnesses and the Coroner therefore summed up for the benefit of the jury. The opposition of the parents to their son's liaison with Kathy had brought about the tragedy. His mother was bitterly opposed to the union. John had married, but had kept that fact a secret in order to avoid a confrontation.

No one would ever know what had taken place that evening, but their deaths had occurred fairly soon after John had returned home at 6 p.m. The postman had seen them both when he had called just after 6 o'clock and the doctor had said, when he had examined the bodies at about 10 o'clock the next morning, that death had occurred at least twelve hours previously.

Mr. Walton then tried to visualise the sequence of events that had taken place that dreadful evening. Mrs. Robinson was probably sitting at the table writing her letters. There must have been some kind of violence displayed in the room by the fact of the overturned chair and also the minor wound described by the doctor which would have bled. For some reason John must have given his mother a glancing blow with some heavy instrument, presumably a hammer, and Mrs. Robinson got up, ran or staggered, as the case may be, and here the Coroner urged the jury to remember the bloodstains found in the hall by the Superintendent. There was the possibility that her son had followed her and had inflicted a very much more serious blow that would have been in itself sufficient, eventually, to have caused death which knocked her over, probably unconscious, to the floor. John had then held a shotgun right against her head and fired it. He then went back along the passage, breaking the gun, which had ejected the cartridge, went into the sitting room and, placing the barrel of the gun to his eye, fired it.

Mr. Walton listed some possible alternatives to this theory but dismissed them as too fanciful. He reminded the jury that evidence had been given of John's uncontrollable temper over the incident of the dog and the possibility of mental imbalance as mentioned by the doctor in his evidence.

The jury were absent for a few minutes only before returning with their verdicts that Mrs. Robinson had been murdered by her son and that he had then committed suicide during the course of temporary insanity.

The sad affair was no doubt talked about for some time before Haversham and its surrounding villages and towns could resume their relative tranquillity.

Life, of course, goes on and possibly, with no sense of irony in mind, the Palace Cinema at Wolverton were now showing the film, 'As Good as Married' for three days and following that, Tyrone Power, Loretta Young and Don Ameche in 'Love is News'.

(1) Not her real name.

"I HAD A FUNNY FEELING SOMETHING WAS WRONG!"

HIGH WYCOMBE – 1960

Many and varied are the explanations offered by someone for murdering another human being. Love, greed, revenge, jealousy, all have been offered as excuses for committing this atrocious crime, but surely one of the strangest reasons ever given was behind the killing that occurred in High Wycombe in 1960.

On the night of Sunday, 23rd October of that year, Mrs. Holderness decided that she would stay overnight with her daughter, Mrs. Kalima. Mrs. Holderness, who was in her late sixties, had been married twice, once to a William Parrott, who had died in 1937, and then to George Edward Holderness. They, however, had separated in 1947 and she had not seen him for several years. Mrs. Holderness now lived in a semi-detached house at 134 Bowerdene Road, High Wycombe, a house that she shared with a lodger, Paul Geis.

He had lived with her for only four weeks and occupied a small back bedroom, whilst Mrs. Holderness used the front room. He was not the ideal lodger, as Mrs Holderness confided to her daughter, for although he was 27 years of age he still wet the bed! When she had mentioned this to him he had been embarrassed by the fact that he was still plagued by what many people considered was a childhood habit and which, at his age, he should have outgrown. Mrs. Holderness also grumbled that she had the additional bother of the mess her lodger made on his mattress.

After staying the night, Mrs. Holderness took leave of her daughter early on Monday morning. "I'll see you on Friday," she said as she left. It was, unfortunately, not to be so. As this was the last time that Mrs.

Views of Bowerdene Road, High Wycombe.

Kalima was to see her mother alive. Later that morning a Mrs. Howard, who lived next door to Mrs. Holderness, was standing at the side door of her house and saw Geis leave by the back door. She watched as he carefully locked it before he walked away.

Some time later a salesman called at 134, Bowerdene Road. Mrs. Holderness was a customer of his and he was surprised when the only response to his knocking was the sound of her dog barking. It appeared to be shut in a room inside the house. The salesman left but returned later the same day and tried again. As before, all that he could hear was the yapping of the dog.

*

Police Constable 658 David Stephenson, of C Division of the Metropolitan Police, was patrolling Wardour Street in London's West End that same afternoon accompanied by another officer, when an agitated man approached him and asked for directions to the nearest Police Station. Politely, the constable enquired if he could assist. The man, who later identified himself as Paul Geis, hesitated then blurted out, "I've killed my landlady and I don't know what to do!" P.C. Stephenson must have been momentarily taken aback, for it is not every day that a policeman is confronted by someone admitting to a killing. The constable then asked where this 'killing' had taken place. "In High Wycombe," Geis replied. "We had a row, I put my hands round her throat and killed her." P.C. Stephenson summoned a police van and took Geis to West End Central Police Station. When they arrived there, Geis was interviewed by Detective Sergeant Ernest Cooke, who asked Geis if he could tell him what had happened. More used to the vice and villainy that went on in the heart of the nation's capital, the Detective Sergeant must have wondered at the strange story that was now unfolded before him. "I have a weakness for wetting the bed," Geis explained. "I got up this morning. Mrs. Parrott, (Geis knew Mrs. Holderness by her previous married name), my landlady came in. She started on about my giving her ten shillings (fifty pence) towards getting a new mattress, but I did not see why I should because I could buy a new one when I left. Well, we had a row. I put my hands above her shoulders and she dropped down dead. I left her upstairs. I went downstairs and the dog thought I was going to take him for a walk, but I shut him in. I had a shave before I left. When I got outside I kept thinking about it, saying, 'My God! What have I done?'"

After listening to this casual confession, Sergeant Cooke telephoned the County Police at High Wycombe and informed them that they had a possible murder case on their hands.

Detective Inspector Michael Whiting, the then head of the Wycombe C.I.D., and other officers went immediately to 134 Bowerdene Road where, as described by Geis, the body of Mrs. Holderness lay in the back bedroom. Both of the detectives could see, and it was later confirmed, that the landlady had been strangled.

Inspector Whiting now made the journey to West End Central Police Station and took Geis back to High Wycombe, where he made a statement under caution to the detective. "She wanted ten shillings from me because she said the mattress was ruined. I said I would buy a new one. She kept on about the mattress. She told her daughter about it when she came and that embarrassed me. I paid her £3. 10/- (£3.50 pence) last Sunday for keep. I had put a shilling (5 pence) in the gas and asked her for the shilling. She paid it and then said I did not pay for the mattress. She came in about half past seven this morning and I asked her for 2/- (10 pence) as I had put on the gas. She said, 'Here it is. I pay the two shillings for the gas but you don't pay ten shillings for the mattress.' I said I would pay when I left because, if I paid ten shillings every time I did it, I would pay for several mattresses. She said I was a cissy and grown men should not wet the bed. She tried to pass me and I said to her, 'Prove to me it's ruined.' She tried to pass me on the landing. I got hold of her shoulder and turned her round. I remember ornaments on the staircase, turning round and swinging about as I went downstairs. I put a raincoat on and had a funny feeling something was wrong. My eyes went blurry when I heard noises upstairs. I next remember being on the train. I was going to see my parents in Slough, but I was in London and I saw a policeman."

One strange thing that was noticed by the detective was that all the time Geis was in custody he kept washing his hands.

Geis was then charged with the murder of Mrs. Holderness. In reply he said, "Only that I am unfamiliar with the name you mentioned."

Committed to Buckinghamshire Assizes, Geis appeared in January 1961 and pleaded 'Not Guilty'. Mr. A. E. James defended him and made no serious challenge to the prosecution evidence. He brought forward a Dr. Davies, who stated that the accused had been under his care since 1956. His father had also been a patient of his, suffering from a severe mental illness, whilst his uncle and aunt had been detained in a mental hospital. His mother, continued Dr. Davies, although not in High Wycombe under his care, had been regarded as 'highly strung'. The doctor also mentioned the fact that Geis suffered from an 'inherent blindness', adding that from the age of 15 he had become more obstructive and quick tempered.

Mr. James, in addressing the jury, pointed out the heavy responsibility they had in a trial for murder. He added that the defence was one of diminished responsibility and he laid great emphasis on the evidence given by Dr. Davies, suggesting that Geis's mental abilities were substantially impaired at the time he had committed the offence.

The jury apparently agreed and reached a verdict of 'not guilty of murder but guilty of manslaughter'.

Paul Geis was sentenced to 15 years imprisonment.

"CHARLIE, YOU BASTARD!"

SLOUGH - 1964

On the late evening of Tuesday, 28th April 1964, the various residents that made up the household at 9, Lake Avenue, Slough, had more or less settled down for the night. The landlord, Amos Jacob, and his wife, Syvil, were already asleep and the lodgers at the house were either going to bed or preparing to retire. Downstairs 32 year old Sylvia Mary Bull had just returned from a late shift at the Mars factory on the nearby Trading Estate. She had slipped out of her working clothes and had put

Scene of the murder.

Scene of the murder.

on a light blue night-dress and was watching television whilst waiting for her boyfriend, Jonathan Lewis, with whom she was currently living, to arrive.

Another lodger at the house, Mrs. Butcher, had heard Sylvia enter the house shortly after 10 p.m., run some water and had then heard the gas 'pop' in the kitchen. A few minutes later Mrs. Butcher also heard Sylvia shout out, "You bastard!"

There was the sound of screaming which shook the quietness of the house and alerted Syvil Jacob, who in turn woke her husband. They both rushed downstairs from where the shriek had come and saw, lying in a pool of blood on the floor of her room, the body of their lodger, Sylvia Bull. Mrs. Jacob gently raised the head of the injured woman who was covered in blood coming from the front of her body as well as her mouth and nose. Sylvia was hardly alive as the concerned Mrs. Jacob attempted to comfort her,but almost immediately she stopped breathing and died in the arms of her landlord's wife.

Other lodgers who had also heard the screaming hurried to the room and saw the terrible sight. One also noticed a bloodstained knife lying in the hall. Mrs. Jacob became aware that the back door to the house was open and assumed that whoever had attacked Sylvia Bull had probably entered and left the house that way.

An emergency call giving brief details of what had happened was put through to Slough Police Station and uniformed officers attended, supervised by Acting Inspector Vivian Jenkins. He also beheld the body of Sylvia Bull and noticed a large gaping wound in her chest over her heart. He felt for a pulse but could not find one. Inspector Jenkins' attention was then drawn to a large, heavily bloodstained butcher's knife lying on the floor.

Next to arrive on the scene were the C.I.D. who commenced enquiries into what appeared to be a motiveless murder.

The senior detective placed in charge of investigating the crime, Chief Inspector Henry 'Jock' Keenan, ascertained that Sylvia Mary Bull had led a fairly exotic lifestyle. Prior to her death and whilst she had been living at his sister's house in Hencroft St., Slough, she had met up with Jonathan Lewis, who hailed from St. Vincent. They had decided to live together and had moved to the Lake Avenue address in February of 1964.

Chief Inspector Keenan also discovered, through questioning, that a man called Kenneth Roustone Howard, a Barbadian, had called at 9, Lake Avenue and had asked for and been given a room. Mrs. Jacob related to the Police that during the course of his first week Howard had mentioned to her that he and Sylvia Bull had lived together for six years but that she had then run away from him.

Sylvia, Mrs. Jacob went on, had confided to her that she had run away from Howard when they had lived at Reading. She had told her landlady that he was no good and had beaten her.

The victim – Sylvia Bull.

66

When Mrs. Jacob had heard that, she informed the detectives, she had made clear to Howard that she had wanted no trouble. Howard had responded that he would leave and he had done so, taking his things and leaving the door key behind. That he had been unsuccessful in obtaining new lodgings became apparent when he returned the next day and asked if he could have his room back. Grateful to be rid of someone she thought was a potential troublemaker, Mrs. Jacob had said, "No!" quite firmly. He had left swearing and saying, "I love Sylvia," adding ominously, "I must get her back."

The Police were, of course, very interested in finding Kenneth Howard and every endeavour was made to trace him. Jonathan Lewis, who knew Howard and was now frightened for his own safety, as he believed that Howard might come after him, was taken around the Slough and Reading districts to see if he could point him out to the detectives. In the remote possibility that Howard had committed suicide, the nearby Baylis Pond was dragged to see if his body was there but it was not.

A search of the room where Sylvia Bull's body had been found revealed a number of letters written by Howard and placed in a wardrobe.

The eminent Home Office pathologist Professor (later Sir) Keith Simpson in the meantime had performed the post-mortem on the body of Sylvia Bull and found that there were two stab wounds in the front of her chest. One of the wounds had entered 9 inches into her body, transfixing her heart. This had resulted in extensive internal bleeding which was the cause of her death. Professor Simpson stated quite categorically that there were no defensive injuries to her hands.

Meanwhile, other enquiries continued and it was discovered that whilst he had lived at Reading, Howard had worked at the C.W.S. Preserves works in that town. The foreman, William Taplin, was interviewed and he said that on the afternoon of 25th April, Howard had asked for a pass-out and had been given one. He had been seen leaving the premises and then, some time later, returning.

It was on the same afternoon that Mrs. Smith, the wife of the manager of a tool merchant's shop in Bridge St., Reading, remembered Howard calling at the shop and buying a knife. He had specifically asked for

Pathologist, Sir Keith Simpson accompanies Detective Inspector
Henry 'Jock' Keenan to the scene of the murder.

one from a display in the shop window and she had to get it for him. She recollected having to use some grease to remove a number of rain spots on the knife as it had been lying beneath a leak from the window. She had wrapped it up in pink paper for Howard and he had paid for it. Whilst she had been getting his change, Mrs. Smith had observed Howard glancing around the shop. He was particularly interested in the choppers and billhooks, and when she handed him his change he was removing them from their showcase and looking at them rather closely. He ran his hand down the blade of one billhook and remarked that he thought it might do the job better.

Mrs. Smith had innocently enquired what he needed it for and Howard had replied that he wanted it to chop bones. He had then left the shop with his knife but without purchasing any of the other items he appeared interested in.

Detective Sergeant Roy Trenter of Reading C.I.D. had gone to 8, William Street, Reading, and searched the room until recently lived in by Howard, and discovered some wrapping paper similar to that used at the tool merchants.

Despite all the efforts of the Police and the publicity surrounding the case, Howard still remained at large.

On Tuesday, 5th May Mr. Roy Henderson Allenby, a stepbrother of the suspect, saw Howard in Goldbourne Road, West London. Allenby told Howard that the Police were looking for him and that he should go to the Police, to which Howard agreed. On the way to their local Metropolitan Police Station, Allenby asked Howard what the trouble was, only to receive the reply, "Nothing."

Detective Sergeant Colin Burgess must have been somewhat surprised when he saw Howard at Harrow Road Police Station. "I have come to give myself up," Howard told him. "I am scared. Me and the girl, we had a scrap and you want me. It was at Slough."

When he had realised what Howard was referring to, Sergeant Burgess had communicated with Detective Chief Inspector Keenan, and that officer and Detective Inspector Phillip Fairweather (later Superintendent) hurriedly made their way to Harrow Road Police Station where they interviewed the suspect.

Howard told the two Buckinghamshire detectives that Sylvia Bull had lived with him for over five years but had left him, first to reside in Hencroft St. in Slough and then at the address in Lake Avenue. Chief Inspector Keenan showed Howard the letters that had been discovered in Sylvia's room when the Police had searched it on the night of the murder.

"Yes," admitted Howard, "I write them. I write to frighten her."

Chief Inspector Keenan next mentioned a further letter that had been found in a jacket at Howard's address in Reading containing an alleged threat by Howard to kill Sylvia, her boyfriend and then himself. Howard admitted that he had written that as well.

He was then asked if he had seen Sylvia on 28th April. Howard answered that he had gone to Slough and had seen her just after 10 p.m. She had, he alleged, taken off her clothes in front of him whilst they had been talking. "I don't know what happened," he told the two detectives. "I read it in the paper next morning. I don't remember. I don't kill her. I know I don't kill her." Chief Inspector Keenan questioned Howard on what had gone on in the room. "Someone came downstairs and she panicked," he replied. "She say, 'Get out! Get Out!'"

Howard then made a written statement in which he detailed that he and Sylvia had lived together in Reading for almost six years; of how, in October or November of the previous year, he had met a girl called Nora who had wanted to come and live with a brother in the same house. He had asked Sylvia to go upstairs to keep Nora company for a while and when she had come back, she had asked if she could accompany Nora when she went with men. Howard added, "I said, 'Why let Nora take you back on the street' but she said, 'I am my own woman, I can do as I like.' She went out every day and night with Nora. I tell her it not good to do that thing. She had another man at High Wycombe that took her round for men."

Howard then told the detectives that Sylvia had gone out one day to visit the Labour Exchange and had never returned, but some weeks later Nora had informed him that Sylvia was at an address in Slough. He had seen her several times and she had, Howard alleged, talked about coming back to him.

On the 28th April he had met Sylvia and had gone back with her to 9, Lake Avenue. Howard continued, "While she was in the room she said, 'John will be here in half an hour.' I heard someone coming downstairs. We both got frightened and I went away. I just walked around London. Oh God, I told the truth. I pulled the knife only to frighten her. I wave knife and I ask her to come back. She say, 'Have patience.' She call me a black bastard. She hear someone. She bang at me. I bang at her and we fall on the ground. I put light out and go away. When I read in papers next day, I get a piece of bottle and try and cut my throat."

After reading over and signing the statement and completing the necessary formalities, Howard was taken to Slough Police Station and then placed before the Magistrates and was eventually committed to a higher court.

In July, Howard appeared at Nottinghamshire Assizes and pleaded 'Not Guilty' to murder. He admitted buying the knife that had been found by Sylvia Bull's body. He had bought it, he told the Court, to cut bones for his dinner. When he had checked to see if it was still in his coat pocket, he had found a photograph of Sylvia Bull and had decided to see her in an attempt to make her come back to him. He had consumed some drinks on the way to her lodgings and they had argued and she had told him to go, as the man she was then living with (Lewis) was coming back. He remembered putting the knife on the bed and they had wrestled, but when she had heard someone coming, he had left. He claimed that as he left the house she had shouted after him, "Charlie, Charlie, you bastard!"

Despite his story and protestations of innocence, however, Howard was found guilty by the jury and given a mandatory life sentence.

CAN I HAVE MY OLD JOB BACK?

RADNAGE – 1970

William Allen Simmons had his own haulage business. He had also sub-contracted for many years for British Road Services, which was situated in Lincoln Road, High Wycombe. In 1970, he was in his late sixties and he informed the depot manager, Stanley Best, that, as a result of eye trouble, he intended to retire. This came as no great surprise to Mr. Best as Simmons had mentioned this several times before.

After Simmons retirement a re-organisation took place at the B.R.S. depot and the deliveries were re-arranged. In the meantime Simmons had had an operation performed which turned out to be completely successful, so much so that he was adjudged able to resume driving. He therefore approached Mr. Best and asked if he could resume delivering in his old district. Mr. Best replied that he did not think that that would be possible because of the re-organisation that had taken place during his absence. Another man, Edward Barry Price, had now taken over the deliveries. Simmons was quite desperate to re-start work and Mr. Best tried to help him by seeing the branch manager. Simmons was really upset and was heard to mutter to another driver during the course of a conversation, "If I can't have it, I'll see that he doesn't!"

On the afternoon of Friday, 30th October, Simmons returned to the depot after making some deliveries and was seen by Mr. Best to be carrying a long object covered by a dirty white cloth. The next day Simmons was again in the B.R.S. office and spoke to Mr. Best about work that was to be done the following Monday. Again Mr. Best noticed the long object that the former sub-contractor was carrying. Price was also present at the time as was another employee of B.R.S., a female traffic clerk.

There seemed to be nothing untoward at all and Best then left the office, as did the traffic clerk a short time after. She had hardly left when she heard a loud bang come from the office she had just vacated and she returned to investigate. As she did so, Simmons came out and brushed past her. The female clerk glanced into the office and saw Price lying on the floor with blood oozing from a terrible head wound. She looked at Simmons for some sort of explanation. He said, "I dropped the gun and it went off!" The noise had also attracted the attention of others and they rushed to the scene. After a violent struggle with Simmons they wrestled the gun from his grasp and hid it. He managed to break free and demanded to know where his gun was.

A 999 telephone call was made to the police and Detective Inspector Ray Tilly, who happened to be the only C.I.D. officer at High Wycombe Police Station at the time, dashed off in a car to the B.R.S. depot as fast as he could. As he entered the depot he had to make an emergency stop to avoid hitting Simmons who jumped in front of the police car. Getting out of his car, the Inspector asked Simmons what he was trying to do. Simmons response was, "Why didn't you run me over? I've done a terrible thing." Some time later he added, "It was an accident. I dropped the gun and it must have gone off."

Detective Inspector Tilly arrested Simmons and conveyed him to the police station in the centre of town and commenced interviewing him. The first, obvious question was what had happened and Simmons replied, "I wanted my old round back. Since I came out of hospital it had been getting me down. I shot him because he was the one doing most of my rounds. He looked at me so cunningly...I shot through the wrapping. He was sitting behind the door. My mind just snapped!" Simmons was later charged with murder.

He appeared at Bedfordshire Assizes where he pleaded not guilty to murder. He elected to give evidence and stated that he had been upset at not getting his old round back when he had returned to the depot in October. It had seemed as though his legs had been chopped off.

He had obtained a 12 bore shotgun from an army officer during the First World War and had used it for shooting rabbits and pigeons. On 30th October of the previous year he had gone to the B.R.S. depot but could not remember taking his shotgun with him. "I must have put the gun in my car. I was mixed up in my mind. I can't remember when I loaded the gun. I must have loaded it during the morning. I remember going upstairs carrying the gun, but why I did it I don't know. I can't remember going into the general office. Barry Price was filling up some delivery sheets behind the door. I remember Mrs. Barr, the traffic clerk, leaving the office. The next thing I remember is a terrific bang. I rushed out of the office. I can't remember what happened to Barry Price. The bang scared me. I did not deliberately fire the gun. I had it wrapped in the cloth. I can't think why I was carrying the gun."

Simmons' counsel asked him if he had wanted to kill Price. "Certainly not!" was the firm reply. Simmons added that he thought he had dropped the gun and might have stepped on the cloth wrapped around it. He had not at any time deliberately cocked the gun, he asserted.

Several senior doctors were called and testified that Simmons was suffering from severe depression that had substantially impaired his responsibility. After some character witnesses had also given evidence, mainly to say that he was not only a much respected man but also that he would not normally hurt a fly, the jury retired and returned with a verdict of 'Not guilty' on the murder charge, although he was found guilty of manslaughter on the grounds of diminished responsibility.

Mr. Justice Roskill ordered that he be sent to Broadmoor for an unlimited period.

DEATH IN THE SUPERMARKET!

CHESHAM - 1971

To most people Saturday means only one thing; the weekly shopping. It must be done on this day, and so, throughout the land, thousands upon thousands of men and women, young and old, throng the streets of cities and towns, jostling each other in their haste to visit as many supermarkets, stores and shops as they can, purchasing the items and commodities they believe that they need to see them through the ensuing days.

On the first Saturday of 1971, Chesham appeared no different to any other shopping centre. There was, of course, the added attraction, or distraction, of the January sales, and perhaps even those who would not normally go shopping went out, either willingly or unwillingly, to see if there were any potential bargains to be had.

So intent were the crowds, that cold January afternoon, that little notice was paid to a 17 year old youth, Robert Noel Trimmer, as he made his way along the High Street and into Waitrose's supermarket. Had anyone looked closely enough they would perhaps have seen that he was carrying a shotgun!

The supermarket was, of course, crowded at this time of the afternoon, as people stocked up on foodstuffs and other items. Trimmer walked from aisle to aisle, peering intently along each one as he did so. Then he saw the person he was looking for. She was pretty 16 year old Gillian Susan Randall, who was busy stacking shelves from a trolley. Trimmer raised the shotgun and took aim at the schoolgirl and part-time shop assistant and fired the gun's five cartridges into her body, killing her instantly.

In the confined area of the supermarket, the repeated roar, as Trimmer fired off the shotgun, must have been deafening, and for a moment or two everyone present stopped what they were doing, stunned into silence. Gillian's lifeless body slumped to the floor in the aisle by the shelves that she had been loading. The trolley, from which she had been taking the goods, stood motionless beside her, the cardboard boxes scattered around her inert body. The blood from her terrible wounds seemed to form a crimson aura around her head. Trimmer dropped the shotgun, his deadly work done, and he was immediately seized by members of the staff and taken to the manager's office, where he was held whilst the Police were called.

One of the first Officers to arrive was Sergeant Arthur Bingham who, having looked at the scene where the murdered girl lay, then made his way to where Trimmer was detained. Sergeant Bingham informed him that he was being arrested and would be conveyed to Chesham Police Station. Trimmer replied, "She was the girl I was in love with. It would not just work out. Someone here told me to lay off."

It appeared that he worked at Waitrose's as well as Gillian and had fallen in love with her. His feelings for her were not reciprocated, however. To most youths that would have been the end of the matter and they would have focussed their attentions on some other girl. Trimmer was not like most other young men, and he conceived the idea that, if he could not have her, he must kill her. Accordingly he applied for and was granted a shotgun certificate, and then bought a single barrel repeater shotgun. On 2nd January, he marched down to the supermarket and callously shot Gillian as she busied herself about her tasks.

When Trimmer appeared at Berkshire Assizes in March, he pleaded guilty to the manslaughter of Gillian Randall on the grounds of diminished responsibility; his plea of not guilty to murder having been accepted by the prosecution. After the facts of the case had been outlined by Counsel, Dr. John Perkins, the Medical Officer at Winchester Prison, said that Trimmer suffered from schizophrenia, and agreed with the Judge that Trimmer could kill if the circumstances arose again.

Mr. Justice Paull commented that, as long as Trimmer was loose, there was a danger that any girl he fell in love with would be shot. It was a sentiment that even Trimmer's counsel found difficulty in disagreeing with. In sentencing him to life imprisonment, the Judge added that he should remain in custody until there was a known cure for his disease, or until the Home Secretary deemed it wise and safe for him to be released.

MURDER ON THE A4

COLNBROOK - 1973

In the early evening of Saturday, 17th March 1973 a number of people travelling along the A 4 Colnbrook by-pass were to witness a strange sequence of events that led to the opening of a veritable 'can of worms'. It would reveal not only murder but also the murky dealings that went on at nearby London (Heathrow) Airport. Smuggling, pornographic material, second-hand car dealing and attempted illegal immigration.

As they sped along the highway, drivers and their passengers noticed two vehicles on the side of the road facing in the direction of Slough. Suddenly there were three loud bangs, which one of the passers-by recognised from his days in the services as being automatic pistol fire. One of the parked cars, an Aston Martin DB6, then veered across the A 4 in a somewhat erratic fashion, finally coming to rest in a hedge on the opposite side of the road.

Several of those who had either seen or heard these incidents stopped and went back to see what had happened. As they approached the by now stationary sports car, they could hear the sound of its engine revving, and see smoke issuing from the rear. One of these curious drivers had left his car's headlights on, and he saw the driver of the Aston Martin slumped over the steering wheel. He was just about to pull the driver from the car when the exhaust, having overheated, caused the grass to catch fire. The fire was quick to get hold and smoke drifted across the road. Despite the obvious danger to himself, Mr. Thomas Mullan, with the help of another witness, pulled the driver from the car and laid him on the grass verge. Another passer-by felt for a pulse but was unable to

The car in which the victim's body was found.

A4, Colnbrook – the scene of the murder.

find any.

Whilst all this was going on, a man, who was parked in a lay-by some 150 yards away filling his van with petrol, observed someone run from a vehicle on the opposite side of the road to the crashed car and then return. He got into the vehicle and drove off past this witness in the direction of Slough. He noticed that it was an A35 van with a noisy exhaust. The witness also saw that the driver of the van had the lights switched off. As the van was driven further down the road they were turned on.

A little while after, some uniformed Police officers attended, and it was assumed that a road traffic accident had occurred, and it was initially dealt with as such. The man dragged from the Aston Martin was taken to Wexham Park Hospital at Slough where he was certified dead.

When the body was examined more closely it was seen that the wounds inflicted were not consistent with those that it would have received as a result of an accident and they were of a more serious nature. As a consequence of this discovery the C.I.D. were informed. The matter was now to be dealt with as a murder enquiry and would be headed by Detective Superintendent Phillip Fairweather.

Barrie Page – the victim.

The deceased had been identified as Barrie Page and the Police learnt something about him. He had been born in June 1948 and was, therefore, 24 years of age at the time of his death. He was employed as a shift supervisor by an aircraft catering firm near Heathrow Airport and was living at 17, Oakfield Avenue, Slough.

He shared this house with Kevin Ambrose Guilfoyle, who was the same age as Page, and who was employed as a pastry cook with another aircraft catering firm.

A post-mortem was performed by Doctor Keith Mant, Home Office Pathologist, who determined that the actual cause of death was due to gunshot wounds. A gun had been fired at close range from above and slightly behind the deceased's left shoulder.

One bullet had severed the spinal cord, which would have caused instant paralysis of the legs, whilst the second had passed through the aorta and the heart. This would have caused

Detective Superintendent Fairweather, the senior investigating officer.

unconsciousness, and death, according to Dr. Mant, would have followed very rapidly.

One bullet was taken from the body. Another found on the passenger seat of the Aston Martin, after having passed through the deceased's body, and yet a further one recovered from the dashboard of the car - together with three cartridge cases found beside the road where the murder had occurred - were all taken for forensic examination. It was ascertained that they were from a 9 m.m. self-loading semi-automatic pistol similar to a Polish military Radom pistol. The Scientific Officer who carried out the forensic examination further stated that the gun had been discharged no closer than one foot from the deceased.

During the course of their enquiries the Police ascertained that Page had spent the night prior to his death with his parents at Hillingdon, Middlesex, and on the morning of his last day alive had taken his father to Heathrow Airport to catch a plane. He had then called on an acquaintance, a car dealer, and they had visited a number of other car dealers in West London until the late afternoon when the two men had arrived at 17, Oakfield Avenue. Page's Aston Martin car, the acquaintance had noticed, was in the garage at the rear of the house. The two men watched television for a while. When the friend left, it was arranged that they should meet later that night at a public house at Heathrow, Page having mentioned that he had to go out early that night and might meet his friend later at the pub. Page's friend then left the house.

In addition to his regular job, the deceased was also in the business of buying and selling cars, sometimes storing them on his company's premises which were situated near to London Airport. In late 1972 Page and Guilfoyle had visited various countries in Europe, and had purchased a number of cars and imported them into England. Page had then gone on holiday to Yugoslavia with a supervisor of an airline and had smuggled cigarettes and spirits into that country. He had also dealt with uncustomed watches brought into this country from abroad. It was thought that Page was also smuggling drugs into this country.

When the Police delved further into Page's background, they discovered, from various people they interviewed, that he was a man who would do anything to earn money. He apparently performed well at his work, but he would also do anything for an 'earner'. He was not above selling a worthless car to an unsuspecting customer if he thought he could get away with it. He was believed to be about to import drugs and would play a confidence trick on anyone even though he was friendly with them, and he had even, it was said, refused to pay the landlord of 17, Oakfield Avenue the rent he owed him. Page also used others as front men in his business dealings whenever he thought that a deal might go awry, so that if there was any comeback it would fall on them and not him.

The Police also investigated the Aston Martin sports car in which Page had been killed. This car had a chequered history. The registration number, FLP 978J, originally led the Police to think that it was a 1970 or 1971 model worth, as it now stood, about £3,000 to £4,000. When they delved deeper into it they discovered that it was, in fact, made up of two cars, of earlier vintage, i.e. partly made up from a damaged Aston Martin with a D suffix and the shell of a recovered stolen Aston Martin with an E suffix. In 1969 these had been bought by a salvage broker and then sold to a motor manufacturer who had built one car from them. After passing through several dealers it ended up, around the Christmas-New Year period of 1972-3, in Page's hands. During a search of 17, Oakfield Avenue a receipt for £1,900 purporting to be for the sale of the Aston Martin to Guilfoyle by another dealer was found. When this dealer was interviewed, he denied ever having signed the receipt. Eventually, another dealer was to tell the Police that he had witnessed Page forging the signature, as he intended to sell the car on. If the buyer discovered that it was not, as it purported to be, a 1971 model, then no blame would be attached to Page as he would claim to be an innocent party to the transaction. It was further alleged that Guilfoyle knew of this and allowed his name to be used, as he would receive a reward when the deal went through.

Guilfoyle, when interviewed later by Superintendent Fairweather, was shown the receipt. He told the detective that he knew about it, adding that if there was trouble with the finance company it would fall on Guilfoyle not Page. For this he was to be paid the sum of £500.

The car in question was to have been sold to Page's manager for £3,000 and Page himself, after settling up with others including Guilfoyle, would have grossed the sum of £1,100, a nice little earner indeed!

Guilfoyle had been seen during the later part of the evening of 17th March, when Police Officers, including Detective Constable Tommy Kidston, had visited 17, Oakfield Avenue. D.C.Kidston informed Guilfoyle that Page was dead, although he did not say how he had come by his death. To this experienced detective, Guilfoyle apparently displayed no emotion whatever on hearing the news. Whilst the other Police officers conducted a search of the house, D.C.Kidston had asked Guilfoyle some questions concerning his relationship with the dead man. When had he last seen his housemate? Guilfoyle replied that

Detective Constable Tommy Kidston.

it would have been about 6.30 p.m. that evening as he returned home from work, and Page had been in the kitchen. He, Guilfoyle, had then fallen asleep and had no idea what Page had done next.

D.C.Kidston asked Guilfoyle to recount what he had been doing that day and he detailed the day's events, which the tall Scottish detective noted. When he had done so, Detective Constable Kidston remarked that at no time had Guilfoyle enquired how Page had died. Guilfoyle now did so, and D.C.Kidston replied that he had been murdered, but did not go into any further details. Again, to the officer's surprise, Guilfoyle did not appear to be unduly concerned. He asked no further questions nor did he show any emotion over the fact that someone he knew had been killed in such a manner as described by the policeman. D.C.Kidston now asked Guilfoyle to accompany him to Slough Police Station where a more detailed written statement was taken from him. This went into how long he had known Page, their activities in the buying and selling of cars, and of their moving into 17, Oakfield Avenue together.

When questioned again about his movements that day, Guilfoyle stated that he had left his place of employment that afternoon driving one of Page's vehicles, an Austin A 35 van. He had given two sisters a lift from the works to their home. He had then stopped for petrol and had driven straight home. He had arrived when Page was there, and he had sat down on a couch and had eventually fallen asleep. He had not heard Page go out of the house. He had woken up, watched television for a while and had then fallen asleep again, until the Police had woken him when they had knocked on the door. He also mentioned that, when he had returned home, he had noticed Page's Aston Martin was parked at the front of the house. (Page's friend had said it was in the garage at the rear of the house.)

The detectives investigating the murder were not satisfied, and he was seen by Detective Superintendent Fairweather. Guilfoyle now told him that he had arrived at Oakfield Avenue a little later than he had originally said. Guilfoyle was allowed to leave the Police Station whilst further enquiries were made.

Kevin Gulifoyle – the prime suspect.

Meanwhile, the murder was attracting media attention and it was even suggested that it was a contract job, carried out by an international smuggling gang. Independent Television on their programme, 'Police 5', devoted one whole episode to it.

The usual enquiries were still being made by the detectives seconded to the investigation, and a week after the murder had been committed, a Police roadblock was set up along the Colnbrook by-pass in case any witnesses who had seen the events of 17th March had not come forward. It was as a result of these investigations that a driver at Guilfoyle's place of employment mentioned a rather curious fact. In February he had been instructed by the catering manager to accompany Guilfoyle while a search was carried out of all the personal lockers at work. Guilfoyle alleged that he had lost a gun! It was the policy, apparently, for a shop steward to be present when such a search was performed, and the driver being that official was therefore requested to be there. No gun was found, but Guilfoyle was most concerned at its loss.

Superintendent Fairweather decided to have another chat with

Guilfoyle, and he admitted that a Walther gun had been stolen from his locker at work, adding that he had found the gun in the rear of a car that Page had purchased in Holland. He also made a long statement, in which he detailed his business arrangements with Page. He also told of Page having a large number of forged £5 notes and suggesting to Guilfoyle that he could earn £50 a day by getting rid of them. They had even discussed visiting seaside resorts and passing them off. He further mentioned that Page had been in possession of a number of Omega wristwatches that he alleged had been smuggled in to this country, and that Page had been dealing in razor blades, coffee etc. with members of the Yugoslav National Airline. Anything in fact that was in short supply in that country. Page had also allegedly shown Guilfoyle some pornographic films which he had attempted to persuade Guilfoyle to sell. He stated that as far as he knew Page was not smuggling drugs.

He then related that in 1972 he, Page, and two others had gone to Holland, where Page had bought two Volkswagens. It was whilst they were driving back to this country that Guilfoyle had found the Walther pistol. He had smuggled the gun through Customs and had kept it in the garden shed until January 1973, when he placed it in his locker at work from where it had been stolen. Guilfoyle detailed other journeys they had made to the Continent to buy cars which were sold in England. After signing this long, rambling statement, Guilfoyle left the Police Station once more.

The next day an anonymous letter arrived at the Incident Room, saying that Guilfoyle had telephoned a Mr. Alcock (1) and that he, Guilfoyle, had said that he intended to frighten Page as he owed him £3,000.

Detectives soon traced the Alcocks and interviewed them. Mrs. Alcock confirmed that at 6.45 p.m. on Saturday, 17th March the telephone had rung at home. When she had answered it, a man's voice had asked for her husband. She had replied that her husband was at football and he should try later. When she asked the caller his name, he had replied, "Kevin," and had then rung off. She had mentioned it to her husband on his return, but as he knew several men named Kevin he could not think who his mysterious caller was.

A few days later, however, as he was filling up his vehicle with petrol at Colnbrook garage, Guilfoyle had seen him and walked over to him. "I wish you had been in last Saturday when I phoned up." Recognition dawned upon Alcock. "So it was you who phoned," he said. Guilfoyle continued, "Yes, then I would have been with you when Barrie my mate was shot." Alcock had looked at him as Guilfoyle added that he would have been his alibi, that he would not have been the number one suspect and taken down to the Police Station on the night of the murder. He did not actually say why he had telephoned Alcock, but he assumed that, as he had previously asked Guilfoyle to obtain a car for his wife, it had been with reference to that.

The Police found this very interesting, and Guilfoyle was seen at Slough Police Station by Superintendent Fairweather and was asked to go over his actions on the evening of 17th March once again, which he did. Superintendent Fairweather then asked if he had made a telephone call that evening. "No," was the unequivocal reply.

The senior detective suggested that he had in fact telephoned Alcock and that his wife had answered. "No I didn't," Guilfoyle said firmly. Superintendent Fairweather carefully played his trump card, telling him that he had a statement from Alcock and read part of it, referring to the conversation that he, Guilfoyle, had had with Alcock and his wife. Guilfoyle burst into tears. "You'll give my sister and mother protection if I tell you the truth, sir?"

When the detective promised that he would, Guilfoyle went on that he had made the telephone call as Page had left their house. Just after he had made the call, three men had entered. One had allegedly pointed a gun in his face and had said, "If you don't want what's coming to your mate, you'll keep your mouth shut." Guilfoyle paused before adding, "Also sir, it was not drugs he was on, it was illegal immigrants." He outlined a plan whereby he would have met an Indian in either Spain or Yugoslavia, to fly back with him to London where they would have been met by Page. The Indian would have been placed in the rear of a van belonging to Page's company and taken from the airport without having to go through Immigration. Guilfoyle was to have received £600 for this venture.   Superintendent Fairweather's reaction was to accuse Guilfoyle of the murder of his housemate, and of making up the story of the three men. Guilfoyle denied it. He then stripped to the waist and showed the detective some bruises to his arms, which he alleged had been caused by the men.

Guiilfoyle next recounted his actions of the afternoon of 17th March, including that his van had broken down on the hard shoulder of the M4, but after a short time he had managed to re-start it. It had broken down again further along the motorway and he had looked at the engine and found the problem, which had been tissue paper attached to the air filter. He had removed the paper and carried on to 17, Oakfield Avenue where he had arrived at 6. 30 p.m. (He had not mentioned breaking down on the motorway in his previous statement to the Police.)   Page had come out of the bathroom and spoken to Guilfoyle, who had mentioned the car that he was buying for Alcock. Page had replied, "You'd better give him a ring and tell him we will have one for Tuesday." Guilfoyle had then found Alcock's telephone number and was dialling it when Page had left the house, calling out, "See you later." Guilfoyle had spoken to Mrs. Alcock, who had told him that her husband was out. He had given his name as Kevin and had rung off. He had just settled down to read, when there was a knock at the door. When he had answered it, two men had pushed him into the living room, had grabbed him by his arms and held him, whilst a third man had entered, thrust a sawn off shotgun into his face and had said, "If you don't want what's coming to your mate, right! Keep your mouth shut, and think on your mother, your sister-in-law and the baby."   The gunman and his two associates had then left the house.

As soon as Guilfoyle had mentioned the trouble he had had with the A 35 van occurring on the M 4, an Officer from the Stolen Vehicle Squad examined the van, but could find nothing wrong with the air filter.

Later the same day, Guilfoyle spoke to another senior detective engaged on the case, Chief Inspector Leslie Bishop. To him Guilfoyle stated that it was drugs that were the real racket and that the importation of illegal immigrants was in reality part of a confidence trick to be played on others. This was not what he had earlier told Superintendent

Fairweather. Nevertheless, the Indian family concerned in the alleged immigrant incident were seen, and they stated quite firmly that the offer of such a deal by Page and Guilfoyle, to bring one of their relations into this country in the circumstances outlined, had been turned down by them.

It was then arranged that photo-fit impressions of the three men who had threatened Guilfoyle should be made by women Police Officers, who performed this duty. Neither of these officers was satisfied that Guilfoyle was describing real persons, and one, Sergeant Sheila Gray, tested Guilfoyle by suggesting features to be added to the impressions, to which he apparently readily agreed, displaying, in her opinion, little interest in the results. Guilfoyle was next taken to the Photograph Album Department at New Scotland Yard where he was shown a large number of photographs of criminals, but he failed to identify anyone who could have been any of the three men who had entered 17, Oakfield Avenue.

Whilst Guilfoyle was at the Yard, Mr. Alcock was seen again by detectives. He told them that, after having been interviewed by the Police over the telephone call made by Guilfoyle, he had gone to work and afterwards had driven to The Golden Cross, a public house at Colnbrook, for a drink. He had encountered Guilfoyle there, and had rebuked him for not telling the Police that he had telephoned his wife on the night of 17th March. He added that he, Alcock, had now made a statement and that, as this was a murder enquiry, he intended to tell the Police everything he knew. Alcock asked why Guilfoyle had not told the detectives about the phone call and he had replied, "I just didn't, that's all."

Alcock had then asked him what alibi he had put forward, to which Guilfoyle had answered, "I told the law that I fell asleep about half past six and never woke up until twenty past nine. It wouldn't have been me, because it takes more than a quarter of an hour to drive from where I live to where he was shot in my old jalopy." That in itself was significant enough, for it showed that, when Guilfoyle had been asked by Superintendent Fairweather if he had telephoned Mrs. Alcock and had at first denied it, he knew that the Police had contacted Alcock and had knowledge of the incident. Guilfoyle did not, however, admit making the call, until the Superintendent confronted him with Alcock's statement.

What Alcock had to say next to the Police was very interesting. He had had, he related, a conversation with Guilfoyle about a month before. Guilfoyle had mentioned to him that he did not receive a good wage and had then said, "Some bastard owes me three grand. He's got the money, but he won't go to the bank and get it. I'm going to get a shooter, hold it to his back, take him to the bank and make him get it out!" Alcock had, he told the interviewing detective, laughed at this outburst and had asked Guilfoyle who it was who owed him the money. He had allegedly replied, "I know him well. He owes it me through car deals. If he doesn't give me the money I am going to put a few shots his way and scare him."

Guilfoyle had also supposedly said to Alcock, "I had an automatic at home but my house got burgled the day before the shooting and the gun went missing." Guilfoyle had then, according to Alcock, added that he was glad the gun had been taken on Friday, as he would have been in more trouble if it had been found in his house. He had then told Alcock that Page had £14,000 in the bank, but that it was frozen, that it was a joint account, and that half of it belonged to him, Guilfoyle. When Superintendent Fairweather heard this he realised that Guilfoyle at least had a motive for killing Page.

A driver who worked for the same company as Guilfoyle, and who knew that he had had a gun stolen from his locker, was approached by him some time after and was asked if he could get him a gun, as he carried a lot of money and needed one for protection. He had taken Guilfoyle to the home of a friend of his, Bell (2), and had been shown an automatic, and a deal had eventually been struck wherein the gun, ammunition, holster and spare magazine had been sold to Guilfoyle for £30.

Superintendent Fairweather decided that Guilfoyle warranted some further questioning. Accordingly, he saw him after his return from

Scotland Yard. The Superintendent asked him if he had purchased a gun from Bell. Whilst he admitted knowing Bell, he strenuously denied buying a gun from him. Superintendent Fairweather then had to read to him the statements made by the driver at his firm and by Bell. Only then did Guilfoyle admit that he had bought a gun, but he added that he had sold it to Page for £60 the same day. The Detective Superintendent was intrigued as to why Guilfoyle had not mentioned this before. Guilfoyle lamely replied that he had not wanted either of the two men arrested for gun running. The evidence was gone over with Guilfoyle, and he was told quite bluntly that he still had not told the Police everything he knew. He replied, "No. I have told you the lot this time. There is nothing more to come."

Guilfoyle, mainly for his own protection, stayed at Slough Police Station that night. He was then questioned the next day, but denied saying the things that Alcock had told the Police. He was then confronted by Alcock and his statement was read through by Superintendent Fairweather. When the part was reached where Guilfoyle had allegedly mentioned that he was owed three grand, Alcock said, "Kevin, you did say that." Guilfoyle now admitted that he had, adding, "It was to support the reasons for getting a gun." When the piece regarding the £14,000 was mentioned and Alcock reminded Guilfoyle that he had also said that, Guilfoyle responded, "I said that because I could not get him a car and made the excuse the money was frozen." After making a long statement to the Police, Guilfoyle was allowed to leave Slough Police Station.

In the meantime, Bell's home had been thoroughly examined and a 9-m.m. cartridge case discovered, also a plank with a hole in it. When the plank had been taken up, the remains of a bullet were discovered. These were taken away to be examined. Later it was revealed that this cartridge was consistent with having been fired by the same gun used to kill Page.

The Police were keen to discover the identities of the three men who had threatened Guilfoyle, and in addition to placing their Photofit impressions in the official publications, Superintendent Fairweather decided to hold a Press Conference at which he showed the representatives of the media the pictures, and gave the descriptions of the men they were most anxious to trace. Whilst informing the Press of the circumstances, the Police officer was careful not to mention Guilfoyle by name. It did not take long for the newshounds to find out the identity of Guilfoyle and his whereabouts, and they attempted to interview him. At first, in this endeavour they were unlucky, but Guilfoyle later met various reporters at a nearby hotel, where he freely spoke to them about his ordeal at the hands of the three intruders.

The next day Guilfoyle was headline news in the national press. Featured on the front pages of the Daily Mirror and the Sun were pictures of him under the headline, 'I saw the A4 killers'. Underneath, in slightly smaller print, glared the words allegedly spoken by Guilfoyle, 'The next bullet will bear my name'. To the reporter from the Sun he talked freely about having one gun stolen from his works and being offered a second gun for a few pounds. "It was too good an offer to turn down," he told the journalist, before continuing, "It's not the sort of thing you pop pigeons off with. It's for popping off at people. Barry had a big foot in a big door at London Airport and I thought the pistol might come in useful."

He then mentioned the three men who had paid him a visit on the night of 17th March. "I'm not saying that one of those men who called was probably his killer, but I am not giving up the second-hand car business. I'll pick it up again soon and just hope that I don't go the same way as he did."

To the Daily Mirror reporter he said, "…obviously they must have had an appointment with Barry, and after leaving me they must have kept it."

When Superintendent Fairweather saw this he wondered why, if Guilfoyle alleged that he had been so frightened of these men, he could not inform the Police of the incident that had occurred at his home for twelve days. He was now revelling in his new found fame. It was bizarre, to say the least.

Another thing that bothered the Senior Investigating officer was the fact that if Guilfoyle's story regarding the three men was to be believed, and if he was the only man who could identify and possibly give evidence against them, he would have expected Guilfoyle to have kept a very low profile indeed. He would have thought that Guilfoyle would have lived anonymously elsewhere, and certainly not have frequented his usual haunts where he was well known. Instead, Guilfoyle just moved back to his parents' home, the location of which the three men must have known, as they had mentioned his mother and his sister-in-law. Nor did he change his place of employment but travelled there every working day, something else which surely would have been common knowledge to a number of people.

Guilfoyle still used the Golden Cross public house at Colnbrook as well. When all these facts were added together, with the publicity that had been engendered by the national press, it would have been expected of Guilfoyle that he would have been very careful indeed. However, it appeared to the Police that nothing seemed to alter his demeanour at all.

Just in case anything untoward occurred on the several days and nights that Guilfoyle drank at the Golden Cross, plain clothes Police officers also attended the public house. At no time did they see Guilfoyle's attitude change in the slightest from being, if not the life and soul of the place, then no shrinking violet either. Certainly from the reports of the detectives who shadowed him, Guilfoyle did not appear to be a hunted man. In fact he seemed to go out of his way to make his escort welcome by buying them drinks in the bar!

As soon as Detective Superintendent Fairweather heard the news that the cartridge found at Bell's house was identical to those found at the scene of the murder, though the actual gun was never found, he decided to arrest Guilfoyle. Detective Inspectors Blackney Chambers and Peter Goldsworthy detained him at his place of employment.

Asked why he was being detained, Inspector Chambers reminded Guilfoyle of what he had said about Page smuggling drugs, and although he had made extensive enquiries he had been unable to find any trace of Page having done so. Guilfoyle replied, "I thought it would put you off the track." When he was cautioned he replied, "What's all the fuss about. I only wanted to lead you away from me, you know. I didn't want to get involved."

When he arrived at Slough Police Station, Guilfoyle was interviewed once more by Superintendent Fairweather, who went over his story again, ending up by telling him that the gun he had purchased had been the same as that which had killed Page. Guilfoyle replied, "I don't know what to say. It looks very tricky for me at the moment. I just don't know what to say." It was at this stage that he was charged with the murder of Page.

Now that his man was in custody, Superintendent Fairweather played a hunch that he had been keeping up his sleeve since Guilfoyle had first come 'into the frame'. Guilfoyle had always insisted that on the night of the murder he had remained at 17, Oakfield Avenue. Now it was decided to check this out more thoroughly. The landlord and the landlady of the Golden Cross, Guilfoyle's most frequented 'water-hole', were interviewed. They both recalled Kevin being there, at least from 8 p.m. when they had come down from their living quarters above the bars, and he had been one of the customers they had greeted. How could they both be certain that it was that night that he had been there and not any other night? It had been the landlady's 25th birthday, and both she and her husband could remember the night very well! Other people, employees of the licensee and customers, also saw Guilfoyle there that evening.

The Police also inspected the bank accounts of the two men. Page was found to have over £2,000 in his account, which, together with the motor vehicles he held at the time of his death, meant he had assets of between £5 – 6,000. Guilfoyle, it was discovered, had debts amounting to over £200 and only £42 in cash.

If Guilfoyle was pressing his housemate for payment of his share of the car deals, Superintendent Fairweather reasoned, the amount that Page had, and the fact that he would not pay-up, was a good enough reason for murder.

A doctor had examined the bruises allegedly sustained by Guilfoyle

The team that solved the A4 murder.

at the hands of the three men who he said had entered 17, Oakfield Avenue and threatened him. The doctor also inspected the Aston Martin car in which Page had been shot and was prepared to say that Guilfoyle's bruises were consistent with a struggle between the victim, Page, and his assailant, in which the attacker's arms had come into contact with the car door frame during the violent confrontation.

Guilfoyle was committed to appear before the Reading Crown Court and in July of the same year, after a seven day trial, he was found guilty on a majority verdict of the murder of Barrie Page. The Judge, Mr. Justice Thesiger said, in passing sentence of life imprisonment, "I agree with that verdict. I feel sure you shot Page."

There was no appeal against the verdict by Guilfoyle.

(1) Not his real name.
(2) Not his real name.

THE KILLING OF BABY JONATHAN

WENDOVER - 1973

All killing is, of course, terrible. The sudden, violent loss of a loved one will be felt by relatives and friends for a long time afterwards, if not forever. When the victim is a child, the sense of anguish suffered by the parents will affect them for the rest of their lives.

In 1972, Mr. and Mrs. Snasdell moved from London to Wendover to a house named Cotsworthy on the Nash Lee Road. David Snasdell worked at the British Broadcasting Corporation and travelled regularly

The victim's home.

to London, while his wife, Vanessa, remained at home. They had one son and it was shortly after they moved that Mrs. Snasdell gave birth to a second, named Jonathan Rupert, on the 29th December. Also living with them at this time was an old family friend, Miss Mary Farr. However, due to the amount of travelling that David was doing, the Snasdells had decided to return to London and had placed their house on the market. A 'For Auction' sign now stood in the front of their house.

On the evening of Saturday, 10th March 1973, while her husband was at work, Mrs. Snasdell bathed and fed her two children and then put them to bed. Placing baby Jonathan in a crib, Mrs. Snasdell closed the large window of his bedroom but left the fanlight window slightly ajar and drew the curtains across. Jonathan was sound asleep. Miss Farr went to her own room and Vanessa Snasdell settled down to await her husband's return.

About the same time that this was happening, Police Constable Haverley was dealing with a very peculiar customer. A woman had called at Aylesbury Police Station stating that she had nowhere to go, as her husband had thrown her out of the family home. To the constable she seemed vague and distant and, when he enquired as to the reason why her spouse had taken such drastic action, she replied, "You can't blame him. Just look at me. I'm a witch. I'm literally thousands of years old!" She kept muttering to herself and then asked the constable, "If I throw myself under a bus, will I still be alive?" She kept repeating that she was thousands of years old and P.C. Haverley, deciding that something ought to be done, telephoned an area officer of the Social Services Department of Buckinghamshire County Council, who in turn contacted the Mental Welfare Officer. Both attended the police station where they spoke to the woman who gave her name as Genevieve Parslow.

After spending some time with her, the M.W.O. got in touch with a doctor, who decided that he too ought to attend the police station, which he did after first conferring with the Senior House Officer at St. John's Hospital at nearby Stone. He was told that, despite Parslow's feelings of death and suicide, there were no grounds for her admission to hospital. When the doctor had a conversation with Parslow he came to the conclusion that she was not suicidal nor a danger to the public and it was not necessary to detain her. After declining the offer to take her back to her home or at least to wait whilst an intercession was made with her husband for money for lodgings, Genevieve Parslow walked out of the police station and into the night.

On Sunday morning, Mrs. Snasdell was awakened at about 9 a.m. by her elder son wanting a drink. This was somewhat unusual, as baby Jonathan often woke his mother for his first feed of the day around 6.20 a.m. to 7 a.m.

Having made a bottle for him, she went into his bedroom and noticed that the curtains were drawn back and the crib, which had contained her baby, was now empty!

Her first thought was that Miss Farr had taken Jonathan in to her room, but this was not so and, with rising panic, Mrs. Snasdell made a more thorough search of the baby's room. When she could not find him, she screamed out for her husband. After making an emergency call to the police, Mrs. Snasdell ran out of the house in a frantic bid to find Jonathan.

The first police officer who arrived on the scene, P.C. Ken Whiteman of the Traffic Department, realised the seriousness of the matter and requested the assistance of the C.I.D., Scenes of Crime Department and a dog handler. P.C. John Burt of the Dog Section responded, and with his dog, Loki, commenced a thorough search around the property, the grounds of adjoining bungalows and fields, initially without success. At this stage there were no large scale maps of the area but P.C. Burt had a set and copies were made and distributed among the searchers. It was then suggested to the officer in charge of the Police Support Group that he use his discretion and make a wider a search of the area. This was agreed to and P.C. Burt wandered further along the road towards Terrick. Perhaps it was sixth sense that made him put Loki to work where he did and he began to walk along the wide grass verge. There was a very deep ditch and a tall hedge that had been cut back, except in one place where there was a small, overhanging tree. Loki went straight into the ditch at this point and when P.C. Burt looked down, he saw the body of a child

P.C. John Burt with his dog, who found the body of the victim.

lying in a few inches of water. It was all too clear to the police officer that there were no signs of life. A post-mortem examination performed later the same day by Sir Keith Simpson revealed that the baby had died from drowning.

A full scale hunt for the abductor was by now in progress and a number of witnesses who had been travelling along the Nash Lee Road in the early hours of Sunday were interviewed. They reported seeing a rather strange figure lurking in the general vicinity of Cotsworthy. It was, of course, imperative that this person be found and, if he or she

100

was innocent of any wrong-doing, be eliminated from the investigation. The enquiries carried on over into Monday, 12th March, with teams of detectives continuing their search for the killer and concentrating their resources in the vicinity of the crime.

Whilst this intensive police activity was going on, Mrs. Norman, a housewife living at a farm in Butlers Cross, who had read about the abduction of Jonathan in the national press, left her house on an errand and happened to notice a woman standing by the gate of a cottage near her drive. Mrs. Norman thought she looked dazed but when she returned a couple of hours later, as the woman was no longer there, she put her to the back of her mind. However, that afternoon, on looking out of her kitchen window, she saw the same pathetic woman now standing in her garden. Mrs. Norman went out to her and enquired if she could be of any assistance. She received the somewhat odd reply, "No! Nobody can." Feeling rather sorry for her, the kindly Mrs. Norman invited the strange visitor into her house for a cup of tea. A bizarre conversation took place in which the odd guest said that Mrs. Norman knew who she was and that she should not be there. Eventually, after some coaxing, the eerie woman then made the astonishing admission that she had taken a baby. Mrs. Norman recalled the report that she had read earlier in the newspaper and now made a telephone call to the police who responded immediately. They recognised the stranger as Genevieve Parslow, the visitor to the police station the previous Saturday night.

She told the police officers that she had gone to Cotsworthy, she recalled the 'For Auction' sign, had reached in through the window, pulled the cot over and had taken the baby out. Parslow was asked what she had done then and replied that she had put him in a ditch and, when he had cried out, had stamped on him! Genevieve Parslow was conveyed to Aylesbury Police Station where, after being interviewed by Detective Superintendent Brian Weight, the investigating officer, she was charged with murder.

Later the same year, when she appeared at Reading Crown Court, Parslow's plea of 'Not guilty' to murder but guilty to manslaughter on the grounds of diminished responsibility was accepted by the prosecution.

It was mentioned, in passing, that Parslow had a history of mental disturbance and had spent some time in a mental hospital. Mr. Justice Thesiger commented, "This is a tragic warning to all those who criticize judges for taking baby snatchers out of circulation in the community." He then made an order under the Mental Health Act, detaining Parslow in Broadmoor for an unspecified time.

THE CLOCKWORK ORANGE MURDER

FENNY STRATFORD - 1973

Fenny Stratford is one of the oldest towns in the county. To the Romans it was known as Magio Vinium and for centuries they tramped up and down Watling Street, the majestic road that runs from Dover to North Wales and on which Fenny Stratford stands. When their Empire waned, as all Empires do in the fullness of time, and the Romans withdrew, the 'barbarians' came to this country; Saxons, Vikings and Normans left their mark and their varied cultures upon the land (1). The names of towns and villages, the institutions and even the richness of the English language today are inherited from our 'barbaric' forbears. Small though Fenny Stratford might have been, and still is, it was an important town in North Buckinghamshire. Watling Street was for many years an important route for the stagecoaches that made their way to and from London and many a coach stopped at The Swan Inn, as well as the others that stood in the village (2). The Grand Junction Canal, constructed in the late eighteenth century (renamed the Grand Union Canal in the twentieth century), passed through the town, but shortly after the end of the Napoleonic Wars Fenny Stratford was described as a '...small decayed market town...' (3). And with the building of the London to Birmingham Railway the steady decline in its fortunes began. The line, which had been expected to run through Fenny Stratford and thence to Stony Stratford thereby following the route of the Watling Street, instead came through Tring and was sited a mile away from the old town at Bletchley, as was the railway station (4).

Gradually, through the nineteenth and twentieth centuries, people built houses and shops between Fenny Stratford and Bletchley towards the railway line and the old town gradually deteriorated, although it has recovered somewhat of late. As Sir Frank Markham states in his two-volume work '…another social change was the twilight or blight that descended over Fenny Stratford and is still there'(5).

In the 1960s and early 1970s it had a general air of being run-down and with the arrival of the 'new city' of Milton Keynes, Watling Street, known to thousands of motorists since the 1920s as the A5, lost even that appellation. It now became the V4, part of the grid pattern of the city, whilst the 'new' A.5 threaded its way through the city from Little Brickhill, to the south-east of Fenny Stratford and Milton Keynes, to Old Stratford, Northamptonshire, in the north-west. Amongst all the changes, some things remain the same. Near the junction of Watling Street and Aylesbury Street, which lies opposite the Swan, is another old building – the parish church of St.Martin's. Both were to play a part in a tragedy that would unfold on the night of Wednesday, 4th April 1973. Leading off Aylesbury Street which, as its name implies points in the general direction of the county town to the south, there are several short streets which run from this road, including Church Street, which is opposite St. Martin's Church, George Street and Denmark Street.

At 60 years of age, David McManus was one of life's losers. From the start he had had to fight against the cruel knocks of life, for he had been born illegitimate in Northern Ireland and no doubt in that province, in which religion did and to a great extent still does play an important part in life, his mother would have to bear the odium of having, and David for being, a 'bastard' child. Not the most auspicious of starts in life. David left Northern Ireland in 1935, presumably to seek his fortune in England, but life in the inter-war years was not much better on the mainland and he drifted from one job to another, all of rather short duration, gradually sinking lower and lower in the social scale of life. He wandered the country picking up what he could, begging if he had no job and, when he had money in his pocket, spending it on cheap drink. He was often arrested by the Police for numerous petty offences such as begging and drunkenness. By 1973 he had accumulated the unenviable record of 46 convictions in various Courts. He was an alcoholic and had stooped so low that he was reduced on occasions to drinking methylated spirits. He was in fact the lowest of the low and no doubt to some people he was considered a 'sub-human', even if they did not actually say that. Often he slept rough, as even the dreariest 'doss houses' refused to accept him now. The only comfort he received was when he was picked up by the Police and spent a noisy night sleeping off his alcoholic stupor in the relative comfort of their cells, preparatory to another brief appearance before the Magistrates.

On Monday, 2nd April 1973 he had been arrested for being drunk and disorderly in the Queensway, the main thoroughfare of Bletchley. Although none of the participants in that particularly squalid action, the offender, the arresting officer, the Sergeant who accepted the charge, the Constables who took him before the Magistrates the next morning and who tried to keep upwind of their odorous companion, the Police gaoler who locked him up in the cells at the rear of the Court nor the Magistrates who fined him the paltry sum of £1 for his previous night's misdemeanour, realised at the time, it was to be McManus' last arrest and appearance before a Court.

Released from the confines of the cells with just twenty pence in his pocket and a few curt words from the Police Officer who was acting as a gaoler, McManus was back out on the streets. It might have been better for him if the Magistrates, instead of fining him, had sentenced him to fourteen days imprisonment. Although this would most probably not have solved his drink problem, it might have saved him coming to a violent and sordid end.

Just a few yards from the Court which, until comparatively recently had also been the local Police Station, McManus stumbled the few yards along Simpson Road in the direction of the Watling Street and The Swan Hotel.

*

On the evening of Wednesday, 4th April, the landlord of The Swan, Stanley Regen, was serving behind the bar when he observed McManus walk in. Mr. Regen took particular notice of this customer as he surmised, quite rightly, that he was down on his luck. In fact he later admitted that had the bar been full he would not have served McManus because of his unkempt appearance. However, when his unwholesome customer asked for a pint of bitter, it was duly poured out and handed over to him and, having paid the sum of 15 pence, McManus sat down in a corner chair by the fireplace. Ian Regen, the son of the landlord, had just made the fire up and McManus commented to him how nice it was to see a coal fire.

Another person who noted the Irishman in the bar was David Westwell, who had been staying at The Swan since March. Westwell had, the previous Sunday, travelled to Brayfield in Northamptonshire to attend a 'banger racing' meeting. He had gone with a youth, Richard Huntley (6), known as 'Dopey' to his friends, and two other young men.

All that Sunday Huntley and the two friends kept talking about a film that had recently been shown at the Studio Cinema in Bletchley, 'A Clockwork Orange'. Directed by the late Stanley Kubrick the film depicted a gang of youths whose sole aim in life was to terrorise people. In the film they had beaten up one man, gang-raped his wife and killed another. (The events depicted in this film, in the early 1970s were extremely offensive to the general public and there was the predictable argument about the violence acted out.) That afternoon at Brayfield 'Dopey' and his friends endlessly played the theme music from A Clockwork Orange on their cassette recorder.

As the evening of April 4th progressed, McManus began annoying the customers of The Swan by cadging cigarettes from them. Mr.Regen warned him about his conduct and when McManus became aggressive he was unceremoniously removed from the premises. He was seen to shuffle off across the main road towards St.Martin's Church and Aylesbury Street. About the same time, Huntley left The Swan as well.

McManus entered the Fish and Chip shop, sited just a few yards beyond the church, and bought a pasty and chips from a part time assistant who worked there. A few minutes later, when the shop closed for the night and the assistant went out to the rear of the shop to collect his cycle, he heard the sound of voices coming from the direction of

*St.Martin's Church, Fenny Stratford, where the
attack on David McManus started.*

the church. Whoever was there also appeared to be walking on broken glass. As he wheeled his cycle around to the street the assistant became aware of someone walking up a passageway between the church and a yard. He watched and observed this person, a youth, go over the wall to the churchyard and into the porchway, peer into it and speak to someone who was concealed from view. The shop assistant then saw that the youth was holding something in his right hand and the assistant watched as the youth walked to the front of the churchyard and adopted a crouching position by the wall. He was certain that the youth was holding a brick in his hand.

The shop assistant rode off on his bike towards home, passing by McManus. He did not appear too steady on his feet, which the assistant put down to the effects of drink. Shortly after, several people either heard the sound of shouting and the breaking of glass or saw McManus staggering along Aylesbury Street. Mr. Dunnett, the manager of Mares, a Gentlemen's outfitters situated on the corner opposite the Fish and Chip shop, and who lived above the premises, was taking a last look out from his lounge window before retiring for the night. He noticed McManus staggering along Aylesbury Street but his attention was also drawn to the fact that the man's head was covered in blood, so much so that Mr. Dunnett could not distinguish his face at all. It was as if, he was to relate to the Police, the man was wearing a red mask shining in the reflective glow of the street lighting.

Mr. Dunnett noticed McManus turn into Fortescue's Garage, a few yards further along the road, and disappear behind the petrol pumps. The next thing he perceived was a youth peering out of the alleyway situated on the other side of the Fish and Chip shop staring intensely after the old man. Suddenly he saw the young man run up and also go behind the petrol pumps. Fascinated by all this, Mr. Dunnett saw that the youth appeared to be straightening himself out from a bending position behind the pumps, holding some object in his hand. The youth then sprinted off along Aylesbury Street.

Mr. Dunnett decided to see for himself what had taken place and went downstairs, out into the street and peered across at the garage. He could see a dark object lying on the ground behind the last petrol pump. He returned to his shop and telephoned the Police.

Another witness to this action was a man who had also purchased some fish from the same shop earlier that evening which he was eating in his car in one of the side roads off Aylesbury Street. He looked across to St. Martin's Church and saw a dark haired youth in the churchyard facing the road. At first he saw that the youth was holding something in his hand but then noticed that he had dropped it. He also glimpsed another young man standing with him. As he consumed his fish he saw McManus walking unsteadily along Aylesbury Street. The silent watcher next observed the youth with dark hair standing outside the Fish and Chip shop looking decidedly agitated, glancing up and down

Fortescue's Garage, where David McManus died.

Aylesbury Street before suddenly running off along the pavement. The witness to this, having eaten his supper, drove into Aylesbury Street and, as he passed Fortescue's Garage, saw the body of a man lying on the ground behind the petrol pumps. He stopped his car a few yards further on and he too telephoned the Police from a nearby kiosk.

*

Several Police officers attended the scene and it was quickly realised that a brutal murder had taken place.

Detective Superintendent Brian Weight (7) took charge of the investigation that involved not only the local Police but also officers from the Regional Crime Squad. The usual extensive enquiries began and during their course, on the afternoon of Thursday, 5th April, Detective Constable Geoffrey Smee of the Reading Regional Crime Squad and Detective Constable Tony Walton of Bletchley C.I.D. went to a building site where they interviewed Huntley. As D.C. Smee told him that they were investigating the murder of McManus, D.C. Walton glanced over

The scene at Fortesque's Garage where McManus died –
notice the police cycle.

Huntley's clothing. He could see several dark red marks along the bottom of Huntley's trousers and, suspecting that they might be blood stains, the two detectives decided that the youth was worth closer questioning than they could give him at the building site. Accordingly he went with them to the Police Station, where in the interview room he was asked to remove his clothing which would be taken for forensic examination.

Huntley agreed that he had visited The Swan on the night of Wednesday, 4th April, adding that he had left on his bike and gone home. He had not, he told the detectives, seen the old tramp leave the premises.

There was a hurried consultation between the senior Police officers engaged on the investigation and Detective Superintendent Weight and

Inspector Hammond, who was also on the case, entered the interview room. He pointed out to Huntley that he had been in the same bar as the deceased. The youth answered meekly, "Yes," and turned deathly white.

Superintendent Weight showed Huntley his trousers which had been taken from him just a short time before. "Your trousers have been examined and they are covered in blood."

Detective Constable Tony Walton arrested the murderer of David McManus.

"Yes, I cut my hand at work," was the lame reply.

"Show me the cut on your hand," Superintendent Weight demanded and Huntley pointed to his left wrist where he had a small scab. The Detective Superintendent was not impressed. "There is a considerable amount of blood on these trousers which did not come from that tiny cut," he pointed out. "Were you in a fight with the old boy?"

There was a slight pause then, "Yes, it was me," he said almost inaudibly.

"What happened?" Superintendent Weight continued, and the detectives in the room listened intently as the youth unfolded a tale of horrific murder.

"I was in the pub with some of my mates and this old boy was in there. The way he was talking to everyone he seemed to be mad. He kept scrounging fags. Then I went out of the pub and got on my bike and met him in Aylesbury Street, by the chip shop. He was carrying his chips and started to pester me for money and I told him to clear off. He got hold of my hair and started to fight. I hit him and he went over the wall and carried on fighting in the churchyard. He got into the church doorway and we carried on there."

Detective Constable Smee interrupted him. "What did you hit him with?" he enquired. "First my fist and then a brick I found in the churchyard," was the answer, before adding, "I used some bottles on him I found in the church doorway."

"Did he hit you at all?" was the next question. Huntley replied, "He pushed me about and pulled my hair."

Superintendent Weight pointed out that, although it appeared to have been a ferocious fight, Huntley did not have any marks or bruises. The youth reluctantly concurred.

He was then asked if anyone was with him when the fracas had taken place. Huntley replied in the negative.

Detective Inspector Hammond expressed incredulity that the horrific injuries caused to McManus had been committed by just one person. "Yes," replied Huntley. "I kept hitting him until he fell into the church doorway."

Superintendent Weight persisted, "Tell the truth. Who else was involved?"

Huntley attempted to look the senior Police officer in the eye. "Look, I know all about grassing but you must understand I was on my own. It would be easier if I had been with someone else."

Huntley then alleged that after this fight in the church he had jumped on his cycle and had ridden off home. Inspector Hammond expressed his disbelief that after the engagement between the two all over the precincts of the church, the striking of McManus and of his retaliation, he managed to do all this whilst still carrying a packet of chips and a pie which the Police found at the rear of the church porch.

Huntley sat and looked at the table before replying, "Yes, but it was as I told you."

It was pointed out to Huntley that McManus had been seen walking from the church yard toward Fortescue's Garage and that when he got to the forecourt a youth had also been observed following him along Aylesbury Street onto the forecourt and behind the petrol pumps, where McManus had been attacked with pieces of house bricks. "The description fits you.... You did it, didn't you?" demanded Detective Constable Smee. Huntley replied, "All right, I was going home down the alley way and when I looked round, the old boy was walking away. I went back to get him... I picked up a couple of bricks and threw one at him. I think it hit him and he fell down. I hit him over the head with the other brick."

"Where did you put the brick?"

"I put it down at the back of the garage just before I climbed over the brick wall."

After hearing this confession to murder, the two senior detectives left the room but returned some time later with the youth's stepfather who said, "What have you been at, lad? This gentleman has told me terrible things."

Huntley answered, "I killed someone... I hit him with bottles and bricks... He kept asking me for money."

Huntley then, in the presence of his stepfather, made a statement in which he described what had allegedly happened that night.

"... I saw this old boy who had been in the pub. He was coming out of the chip shop walking towards me. When I got near him he asked me for some money and I told him to go away. He grabbed me by the arm and I pushed him off. He got hold of my hair and I turned round and hit him with my hand... And we started to fight. I hit him and he went over the wall into the churchyard... I got over the wall to hit him again... He started backing off into the church doorway... And I knocked him down on the church seat with my fist... I picked up a piece of brick and threw it at him. It hit him. He went onto the floor and when he was getting back up I hit him with two milk bottles that I found in the doorway. I hit him on the head. I ran off... I looked back when I reached the corner and I saw the old boy going out of the churchyard. He seemed to be looking for me... I walked up the street and saw him on the forecourt of the garage. I picked up these two bricks and threw one at him. I think it hit him. He was still standing up and I hit him on the head with the other brick. He fell down and as he was going down I kicked him on the

The porch of St.Martin's Church.

side. Then I ran off, leaving him on the ground... I went back and got my bike and went home... When I got home I noticed I had some blood on my trousers. Then I went to bed."

After recounting this terrible story of murder, Huntley was charged with the crime and was brought before the court and remanded in custody.

The following week when he reappeared at Bletchley, Huntley saw Inspector Hammond and said that whilst he had been in Bedford Prison he had been thinking and felt that he ought to tell the truth.

In this second statement Huntley related how he had seen McManus coming out of the chip shop and go into the church porch. "... I followed him there because I was going to nick his cash off him. He was sitting

The porch of St.Martin's Church.

down in the corner eating his chips. I asked him if he had any money…
He only had one and a halfpence there. He asked me if I had got any
money for him and I told him to get stuffed. He grabbed me by the arm
and I hit him with my fist and knocked him back against the wall. Then
he hit me back and I stumbled backwards. I turned round to run off
and I saw a bit of paving stone… and I threw it at him. It hit him and
knocked him down on the floor on his knees. He started to get up and
I saw these two milk bottles… I hit him with one and I turned to run
away and I threw the other one at him… The old boy came out of the
church, looked around and started walking up Aylesbury Street… And I
came back after him. I followed him up the road and he went onto the
forecourt of Fortescue's Garage and I ran up and got two bricks from

a pile at the back of the garage… I threw one of them at him and I ran towards him and hit him with the other one. As he was falling down I kicked him in the side. Then I ran off, climbed the wall, went back along the alley and got my bike …"

Huntley appeared before the Magistrates' Court represented by local solicitor Mr. R.H.G.Corner (now H.M. Coroner for Milton Keynes) and was committed to Oxford Crown Court, where in July the same year he pleaded guilty to the murder.

Mr. John Owen Q/C., prosecuting, presented the sordid facts of the case, making reference to the film 'A Clockwork Orange', adding that the murder may have been carried out as a result of it. "If this is so," he added, "the prosecution are bound to say the makers of that film have much for which to answer."

Mr. Owen continued that on the Sunday before the murder took place, a group of young men, including the defendant, had been discussing the film; indeed all the young men that day had thought it was great. They thought the sex as well as the violence had also been great.

"It's not possible to say what part if any was played by that film in the events of Wednesday night (4th April)," went on Mr. Owen. "They may very well have played a very considerable part. It may be significant that the film deals in fact with an attack on an elderly meths drinker. It may be significant that on the Sunday, the accused was apparently approving of the violence in that film and talking about it. It may even be more significant that after the attack the accused himself made reference to that film."

Mr. Owen then went on to outline the facts of the case, remarking that when the Police had interviewed Huntley the next day he showed "… an extraordinary lack of emotion, no feeling." When taken to the Police Station Huntley had confessed to the crime adding, "…Have you seen the film? A friend was talking about it the other night. He saw it, I didn't. It was about beating up an old boy like this one."

"When he had been asked which film he was referring to, the youth had replied, 'Clockwork Orange'. The irresistible conclusion is that it is the influence of the book. Many people have much to answer for, whether they are authors, film directors, television producers or those who allowed these films to be shown. It has produced a cancer among the impressionable young, which all reasonable people desire to be stamped out at once.

Huntley's defence counsel, Mr. Roger Grey Q/C., addressing the Judge, asserted that it was a perplexing murder. "There was nothing in the boy's past or upbringing to account in any way for the brutality he had shown." Mr Grey enquired, "What possible explanation can there be for this sudden gust of savagery?" Continuing, defence counsel said, "There can be no explanation other than the evil influence of this book or the book and the film…It seems that momentarily the devil was planted in this boy's subconciousness. The link between this crime and sensational literature, particularly 'A Clockwork Orange', is established beyond doubt." He then produced Huntley's school report in which his headmaster had noted that he '…showed an unusual addiction to sensational literature of the worst type'.

Mr. Grey finally added, "This boy must face his punishment but he is truly a victim of this indiscriminate portrayal of violence without thought for the consequences. Many people," he added, "have been irresponsible here. Whether authors, film directors or television directors."

The Judge, Mr. Justice Ashworth, in sentencing Huntley to be detained indefinitely, commented, "The length of the order will depend tremendously on you…It will depend on whether you can satisfy the Prison authorities or doctors that you are indeed over this appalling incident. I am convinced you were play-acting in the most horrible form. It must be quite a time before the authorities are sure you are safe to be released."

Of course a furore broke out regarding the film, and the killing of McManus became forever known as the 'Clockwork Orange Murder'. The argument was fuelled just a few days later when another Judge sitting at Manchester Crown Court also criticised the film when he sentenced a youth who had dressed like a character from the film and had then attacked another young man. "Cases like yours present in my view an unassailable argument in favour of a return, as quickly as possible, of some form of censorship to prevent this sort of exhibition being released on the screen or stage. If that happens it will be very salutary to those salacious creatures who appear to determine what appears to be show business today and who would be compelled to earn a more respectable and honourable livelihood instead of exciting young persons to violence at the expense of their victims." (8).

Members of Parliament censured those who made films of such horrific content, as did Mary Whitehouse on behalf of the National Viewers and Listeners Association.

In the end, Stanley Kubrick decided that the film would not be shown again in this country, certainly not in his lifetime. It was suggested that he withdrew it because he was 'tired of the moral panic it caused'. Although, since his death in 1999, it has been put forward that Kubrick may have been concerned that he would be pestered, or worse, by people imitating the characters in the film he had directed.

As soon as Kubrick died, however, the film was re-released and the old arguments resurfaced, although not quite as noisily as they had nearly thirty years before. This perhaps tells us something about the state of society nowadays (9).

*

*

(1) Even today the odd Saxon skull is still found within the parish boundaries.

(2) 'The History of Milton Keynes' by Sir Frank Markham.

(3) 'Tour of the Grand Junction Canal' by John Hassel – 1819.

(4) 'The History of Milton Keynes' by Sir Frank Markham.

(5) Ibid.

(6) Not his real name

(7) Later Chief Constable of Dorset Police.

(8) Mr. Justice Bailey.

(9) In 2001, two youths, one aged just 13 years of age, the other 16, were convicted of killing a tramp by stuffing firelighters in his beard, pockets and shoes as he lay sleeping. He awoke to find himself in flames and died later in hospital.

AUTHOR'S NOTE.

I have often wondered how, exactly, Huntley's name came into the 'frame'. No-one involved in the case could tell me and it seemed as though it was going to be a mystery forever. Then, in 2005, I was interviewing retired police constable Patrick Alfred William 'Pat' Kenny, recording his reminiscences as a policeman spanning the years 1950 to 1986. During the course of a very interesting interview Pat reminded me that for some years he had been area beat officer for Fenny Stratford, in fact from 1972 until March 1977. I mentioned that it was during the time when the so-called 'Clockwork Orange Murder' had taken place. Pat then related his part in the murder investigation.

He had been on duty the night that the murder had taken place, from 5p.m. till 1a.m. Half-way through his tour of duty he encountered the duty sergeant and another constable. They had then received a call to say that there had been a report of a man badly injured in Aylesbury Street, Fenny Stratford, and that he could be dead. The three policemen made their way immediately to the area. When they reached the location they saw the body of David McManus in Fortescue's Garage. A quick inspection revealed that his head had been battered and there was blood all around. "The wheels were set in motion for the powers that be, the C.I.D., the scenes of crime officers and a Home Office pathologist to come out," Pat related, as well as the duty senior detective, Superintendent Brian Weight. In the meantime the uniformed officers went about conducting their own initial enquiries. Pat and his colleague, Police Constable Alan Anderson, visited The Swan where they were told that the tramp had been in there that night, as had three youths who had been dancing around him, making fun of him. Further enquiries were made at the fish shop. The servers confirmed that McManus had called there and had bought pie and chips. The remnants of that last meal could be seen lying scattered around. One also said that when he went outside there had been some youths mocking and teasing him. Pat and his colleagues were continuing with their enquiries when the driver of a car pulled up and the driver asked them what was going on. When he was informed that the police were investigating a potential murder, he mentioned that as he had passed by earlier he had seen three youths on the forecourt of the garage. He had then seen two of them leave and walk in the direction of Manor Road, but he had seen one of them pick up a brick and walk back down towards the traffic lights.

It was at this point that the C.I.D. arrived to continue with the enquiry. Pat asked his inspector, John Humphries, if he could return to duty the next morning to assist in any way he could. It was by now 4 o'clock in the morning. Inspector Humphries agreed to this and Pat cycled home, grabbed a few hours sleep and resumed at 8.30a.m., just as the initial briefing of the teams finished. Pat asked Detective Superintendent Weight if, as the local policeman, he could assist in any way. Mr. Weight told him to go on to his beat and make enquiries as he, Pat, knew not only the area but the local people.

Pat returned to the scene and reasoned that after attacking the old man his murderer had left the scene by way of the footpath that led to Walnut Drive, a road on a local estate. He therefore started knocking on doors there, asking if any of the householders had seen or heard anything suspicious the night before. No-one had and he was beginning to think that he was wasting his time when he encountered a lady who lived on the estate and whose family he knew quite well, though not for criminal matters, it must be said. Pat told her what had happened the night before and she volunteered the information that her son always took their dog out for a walk late at night and usually met a youth he knew from school. The two would normally stop and have a chat, but the previous night he had run past her son without saying a word, which her son had thought was very strange. The mother told Pat the other boy's name and Pat also knew that family. He went to their house immediately and knocked on the door but received no reply. A neighbour told him that the whole family was out. On asking where the son might, be Pat was told that he was working on a certain building site in Bletchley. Pat returned to the incident room with this information. Superintendent Weight not being there, he left a message to be given to him immediately he returned. Continuing with his enquiries around his beat, Pat received a radio message later that afternoon saying that all investigations were to stop as the offender had been arrested and charged. Pat found out then that the youth whose name he had written down was the offender and that where Pat had said, in his message left for Mr. Weight where the youth was working, was where the detectives had found and had initially interviewed him before detaining him.

It is my belief that the information gathered by Pat Kenny, related to me all those years later, led directly to the offender being interviewed, arrested and ultimately charged for this crime.

Pat was a conscientious policeman who went about his work in a quiet manner and was utterly reliable. He was respected by all who knew him, from constables to chief superintendents, from members of the public to coroners, and the above shows the value of a good 'copper' knowing the beat for which he is responsible; getting to know the people, gaining their trust and going about his business without fuss.

Another interesting matter came to light when I was talking to ex-Detective Inspector John Hayward about this murder. He recalled that as a young detective constable he had been given the task of visiting all the cleaners in the area. This was on the morning following the murder. He was told at the one nearest the scene of the murder that a young man had, that very morning, dropped some clothing off to be cleaned which was covered in blood. When he asked to whom the clothing belonged he was told that it was Ian Regen, the son of the proprietor of The Swan. D.C. Hayward had then gone hot-foot to that establishment and had spoken to young Regen. Not getting a satisfactory answer from him, the detective took him to the police station for further interviewing. It transpired that he had had a row with his father the night before which had led to blows being exchanged. Hence the bloodstained suit of clothes which he had taken to the cleaners the following day. When this had been verified, he was released. Some coincidence!

LOVE THY NEIGHBOUR?

MARLOW - 1978

In his book, 'Three Men in a Boat', Jerome K. Jerome, in relating an excursion along the River Thames in the nineteenth century, described Marlow as '...one of the pleasantest river centres I know of. It is a bustling, lively little town...' Over one hundred years later, traffic apart, it is still a very attractive place. The view from the riverbank of the Suspension Bridge and the parish church with the Quarry Woods as a backdrop is one of the most enchanting sights along the whole river and one that enthrals thousands of visitors to Marlow each year. On a fine summer's day, to stroll through the town and along the towpath by the majestic Thames, with boats cruising lazily up and down the river, is surely one of life's delights.

Unfortunately, there is, of course, a downside and Marlow and its environs have witnessed some horrific murders, which have shown the latent beast within man.

*

In April of 1978, Detective Superintendent Keith Milner of the Thames Valley Police was stationed at High Wycombe (1). On Monday, 10th April he received a message that an elderly lady had been found murdered at her home in Oxford Road, Marlow. Mr. Milner, who had played a prominent role in many major criminal investigations, hastened to the scene.

Upon arrival, he was shown the bloody body of 66 year old Doris Hewitt, a spinster who lay face down over a chair in a bedroom. Superintendent Milner could see that the old lady had died after being

The Street in Marlow where murder took place.

stabbed many times. After he closely examined the horrific sight and the Scenes of Crimes officers and photographers had performed their work about the house, Mr. Milner instructed that the corpse of the lady be removed to the mortuary.

With the late Detective Inspector Norman Robson, the Superintendent went to Marlow Police Station where the waiting teams of detectives were briefed and given their various assignments, in an effort to trace the murderer. The two senior investigating officers now drove to the hospital mortuary where they watched as Professor Keith Mant (2) performed the post-mortem examination on the victim. As they observed the Home Office Pathologist carry out what most people would think is

Detective Chief Superintendent Keith Milner Q.P.M., Senior Investigating Officer on the Marlow murder.

a somewhat grisly task, Professor Mant suddenly paused and, looking over his pince-nez glasses at the two detectives, casually remarked, "You know, the last two murderers I've dealt with have been the next door neighbour." The pathologist smiled and the two detectives, grateful for this aside during the gruesome operation they had perforce to witness, chuckled and cast the utterance to the backs of their minds.

Professor Mant confirmed the wounds that had been inflicted upon the dead woman and Superintendent Milner wondered where the weapon was that had killed her. It occurred to him that it may have been discarded in the rubbish bin which had since been emptied and taken to the gigantic tip where all the garbage collected for the area was deposited. The thought of having to search that dump for a knife appalled the detective. The number of men it have would have needed to go over it minutely was a logistical nightmare. Looking for the proverbial needle in a haystack seemed comparatively easy.

At the conclusion of the post-mortem, the two senior detectives returned to the Incident Room at Marlow Police Station to see how things were progressing. It was later that same night that Detective Sergeant Roger Mayne, who had been engaged in house to house enquiries, approached Mr. Milner. "Guv'nor," he said, "I don't like the look of the next door neighbour." Both he and Mr. Milner had a long discussion at the end of which the superintendent had made up his mind. "Go and bring him in and we'll have a chat with him," he said.

It was by now midnight and it was decided that the other investigating

124

teams had done enough for the day and were told to stop, go home and return the next day to resume their enquiries. Superintendent Milner and Inspector Robson remained on duty waiting to speak to the man that Sergeant Mayne had reservations about. When the sergeant returned to the police station, he had with him 28 year old John Woodburn of Oxford Road, Marlow. The two senior police officers then interviewed Woodburn and went over the story that he had related to Sergeant Mayne.

Woodburn insisted that during the afternoon of Sunday, 9th April he had been working on his car. After a while Woodburn was left alone whilst Superintendent Milner and Inspector Robson compared notes. Neither was satisfied with the man and it was decided to re-interview him.

The detectives re-entered the room where Woodburn sat and started going over his story once more, probing any inconsistencies they came across. They went about their questioning quietly and deliberately. Again Woodburn stuck to his story; in fact, he added, he had only spoken to Miss Hewitt when she had asked him for advice on damp in her house. He could be now under no illusion as to the depth of suspicion under which he was held. Woodburn was told to sit quietly and think things over. Finally, one of the detectives remarked that Woodburn must know what they were all thinking and that the only remaining question was "Why?" Woodburn responded, "I don't know why. It was like a dream. I just stabbed her. I just went in there and heard her upstairs. It sounded as though she was sweeping. She said, 'What do you want?' and I stabbed her."

Woodburn then made a statement which was carefully written down at his dictation in which he stated that his wife had been on duty at a local hospital and that he had had a lot to drink. He had returned home where he had made a large omelette consisting of twenty eggs which he had then consumed. He had suddenly rushed to Doris Hewitt's house and had repeatedly stabbed her in the chest and had also plunged the knife in her back four or five times. "There was no reason for it being Doris," he said. "I didn't dislike her. I've felt like this before but I've always taken it out on the car and driven and driven. Sometimes it seems to happen when I go off to sleep and I wake up sweating." Woodburn also produced the knife which he said he had used to kill Miss Hewitt, to the intense relief of Superintendent Milner. He was then duly charged with murder.

*

At Reading Crown Court in October of the same year, he pleaded 'Not guilty', and Mr. John Archer Q.C., the prosecuting counsel, in outlining the case, told the Court that the murder had been committed on Sunday, but the body of Miss Hewitt had not been discovered until the following

The Crown and Anchor public house, where the murderer drank.

day. The prisoner had given himself away in a conversation he had had with the police. During the course of their initial investigations, Woodburn and his 'common law wife' had been interviewed as a matter of routine. That same evening Woodburn and his partner had gone for a drink at the nearby Crown and Anchor public house where the detectives, who had questioned them, were making enquiries among the customers. When they had concluded, Woodburn had followed them to the door and had remarked, "I suppose you don't want me to say anything about her being stabbed?" When one of the detectives had asked him how he had known that Miss Hewitt had been stabbed, Woodburn had replied, "Well you told me!" Mr. Archer looked across the courtroom at the jury and laid great stress on his next few words. "But when the detectives had visited the Woodburn home, all they had said was, 'Your next door neighbour, Miss Hewitt, has been found dead and we are treating it as a murder enquiry.'" The implication being that only the police and the murderer could possibly have known how Miss Hewitt had met her death. Detective Sergeant Mayne had then conveyed his doubts about Woodburn to his senior officer.

"Woodburn," continued Mr. Archer, "...had been taken to Marlow Police Station where he had been interviewed and had made verbal and written statements admitting the murder." After the admissions, Woodburn had gone with the police officers to his home and had produced a kitchen knife from a drawer which, it was the prosecution's contention, was the weapon used to kill Miss Hewitt. The knife had been washed but, continued Mr. Archer, under forensic examination, bloodstains could still be discerned on the blade. Professor Mant had also inspected the blade and he had concluded that it matched the wounds that had been inflicted upon the hapless victim.

All the witnesses for the prosecution were heard and, ultimately, John Woodburn walked from the dock to the witness box to give evidence. He said that he had confessed to the police because he was on the verge of a nervous breakdown and they had told him that he would be able to get treatment in a mental hospital. He had discovered the body of Miss Hewitt, he told the court, but was too frightened to report it to the police in case they tried to 'pin it on him'.

Recounting his actions on the day of the murder, Woodburn added that he had made lunch for himself and had then started work on his wife's car, but during the afternoon he had had to go back inside the house to look at the maintenance manual. When he had gone out again he had noticed that Miss Hewitt's door was open. He had thought that something was wrong because it was very unusual for her door to be open, especially for any length of time. He had knocked on the door, he explained, to see if she was alright but there had been no reply. He had entered the house but had found no sign of her at first. He had walked upstairs and, after checking the front bedroom, went into the back bedroom where he had seen Doris slumped over a chair. He had looked to see if she was alive and had seen some marks on her back. "I thought," he told the hushed court, "she had been stabbed. I checked her heartbeat. There was none that I could feel."

The jury was out for two hours before returning with a verdict of 'Guilty'. Mr. Justice Purchase told Woodburn that he had committed a murder that was callous, indifferent and brutal on an elderly woman with whom he was hardly acquainted. He then sentenced Woodburn to life imprisonment.

*

Detective Superintendent Milner, when he had obtained Woodburn's confession to this atrocious murder, had telephoned Professor Mant's secretary requesting that the pathologist be informed. Recalling Professor Mant's remark at the post-mortem, Mr. Milner requested, tongue in cheek, that perhaps the next time the pathologist could be more precise about the murderer and tell him on which side of the victim the neighbour lived!

(1) Keith Milner is the son of a North Riding of Yorkshire police officer and was later to become Detective Chief Superintendent of the Thames Valley Police and to be awarded the Queen's Police Medal.

(2) Professor Mant died in 2000.

THE 'FAWLTY TOWERS' MURDER

WOOBURN GREEN – 1979

It was to have been a pleasant night out for the friends at the Wooburn Grange Country Club one Saturday in March 1979. There were six of them just having a few drinks. Roy Gray, Robert Jenner, Alan Sykes, Lawrence Tunbridge and two girls, Helen Tucker and Wendy Lowe. The country club, whose exterior had been used when the B.B.C. had filmed the 1970s comedy series, 'Fawlty Towers', was a favourite amongst the young population. Unfortunately, this particular night, there had been trouble. Some fighting had broken out and the six friends watched, but wisely made no effort to interfere.

One of the protagonists, John Warren, who seemed to have suffered

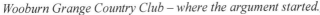

Wooburn Grange Country Club – where the argument started.

the worst of the fracas, had been hit in the face by another participant and had staggered away shouting, "Next time I'll bring a gun!" To which his assailant had responded by shouting at him to get one, adding in no uncertain terms what part of Warren's anatomy he would place it if he showed up with one. Having thus been humiliated, Warren and his friend, Terrence Chamberlain, left the Country Club in Chamberlain's car, a white Ford Cortina.

Eventually Roy Gray's party left in his Morris Minor saloon, just as Chamberlain and Warren returned in their car. It was all a bit cramped in the Minor, with Roy driving, Lawrence in the front passenger seat with Helen on his lap and the others in the back but, when you have had a good night out and a few drinks, who cares? Roy had noticed a white Ford Cortina following him for a while but was not particularly bothered and, as he stopped his car outside Alan Sykes' house in Holtspur Avenue, Wooburn Green, the Cortina also pulled up in front of their car.

Roy and Lawrence saw the passenger of the Cortina get out of the car and run back to them. What was alarming was the fact that for some

The street where the murder took place.

reason he was wearing a gun belt over his shoulder. Roy wound down his window and commented, "Hello, trouble." As he did so, the man swore at him and suddenly shot Roy in the face. He then walked back to the Cortina, jumped in and the car roared off. Roy fell onto Lawrence's lap and both he and Wendy Lowe felt for a pulse. At first Lawrence thought he had discovered one but, with the massive injuries inflicted on Roy's head, death must have been instantaneous.

The party of friends were shocked and horrified at the events that had taken place so quickly and the police were hastily summoned to Holtspur Avenue and the situation was hurriedly explained to them. A description of the car involved in the shooting was given to them and circulated, and later that night the Cortina was stopped in Cippenham, near Slough, and Terrence Chamberlain was arrested. Enquiries revealed that the passenger had been John Warren, and armed police quickly surrounded his house and detained him as well.

Chamberlain told the police that Warren was convinced that the driver of the Morris Minor they had seen leaving the Country Club was the same man who had kicked him in the fight earlier that evening. He continued, "I said he couldn't be positive. He said he was positive, so I followed the car."

Both men were charged with the offence and, later the same year, appeared at Reading Crown Court, where Wendy Lowe, who was naturally nervous as she began her evidence, insisted that she had seen Warren pull the trigger of the gun.

The pathologist who had examined Roy Gray's body had stated that there were no injuries to Gray to suggest that he had been involved in a fight prior to his death. The friends of Roy Gray and the participants in the various fights that had taken place at the Country Club, all stated that Roy had not taken part.

A forensic scientist, who had examined the gun used in the attack, asserted that it needed four pounds of pressure to release the trigger which would not have gone off accidentally.

Chamberlain, when he gave evidence, said that he had tried to break up the fights at the Country Club in which Warren had become embroiled.

He had taken Warren to his home in Stanhope Road, Cippenham, where Warren had collected a shotgun and some cartridges and had told him, Chamberlain, to return to the Country Club, saying, "They ain't going to get away with that!" Chamberlain continued, "I said, 'Don't be bloody stupid.'" Warren had reiterated, "Take me to the bloody Grange!"

Chamberlain admitted driving him back to the club because he was frightened and he did not think that there was anything he could do to get rid of his unruly passenger. "I thought the best way was to play along with whatever he said." Chamberlain had returned to the Wooburn Green Country Club hoping, he informed the court, that it would have finished and that all the people had gone home.

"When we got to the club, Warren saw a Morris car and identified the driver as the one who had kicked him last. I told him there was no way anyone could see who was in which car but he, Warren, was positive and he told me to follow the Morris."

When Chamberlain had remonstrated with him that he could not be certain that he had picked out his assailant, Warren had shouted at him, "Just follow the bloody car!" "I didn't think I had any option but to do as Warren said," Chamberlain added. "I wasn't prepared to be a party to any violence or threats. I didn't want any more trouble..."

He had, therefore, followed the Morris Minor to Holtspur Avenue and, when it had stopped, Warren had told him to pull up in front of it. "He got out of the car leaving the cartridges on the floor. I didn't see him load the gun...I waited in the car with the lights on. I heard a whoosh or fast wind noise. It didn't sound like a gun going off to me. Warren got back into the car and told me to get off out of here, which is what I did. He said he had shot the bloke. I think he said he had shot him in the neck. As we drove past the Morris I checked that the lights were on. I think they went out for a minute."

Chamberlain had then taken Warren back to his home in Cippenham and they had both had a coffee while Warren had cleaned the gun. Afterwards, Chamberlain said that he had driven to Slough Police Station to tell the police what had taken place but had lost his nerve and had then driven to his fiancée's house but it had been in darkness. He had been driving to another friend's house when he had been stopped by the police and arrested.

Chamberlain left the witness box and it was now Warren's turn in the witness box. He asserted that he only meant to frighten Gray and his friends and had no intention of shooting at them or of hurting them in any way. He then told the court about the fights he had become involved in at the Country Club where he had been hit by someone. "I intended to go to the hospital but a friend took me home where I wanted to change my torn jumper. As I was getting changed I spotted the gun in the corner and it came to me it would frighten the people who beat me up. I picked it up. The cartridge belt was wound round the barrel. I got into Terry's car. I told him to take me back to the Grange. When I got back I saw a Morris parked in the entrance. I recognised the driver as the last person who had kicked me. I asked Terry to follow him down the road. The next thing I remember is Terry pulling up past him. I loaded the gun as I pulled up, the Morris was packed with people. I loaded the gun because of the number of people in the car. I thought they might get me. I was just going to frighten them, just swear at them or something. I walked back to the Morris and put the gun through the window. I wasn't pointing it at anyone. I didn't intend to injure or harm anyone. I said something like, 'Kick me now!' to the driver. As I said that, I was starting to bend down to talk through the window. At that point I had aimed the gun towards the windscreen and dashboard. The gun went to the left and someone grabbed it. I didn't see who. It was too dark and happened too quickly. I went to grab the gun with my other hand. The butt of the gun went upwards. I went against the car myself. I was trying to get the gun back. It felt like someone was holding it. The gun discharged then. I wasn't aware of pulling the trigger. My finger was inside the trigger guard. I got back into Terry's car and said, 'Get the hell out of here!' I just wanted to get away before anyone got out of the Morris."

For a moment or two there was a hush throughout the court as those assembled took in the story of how a young man had met his sudden and untimely death on that fateful March night.

Mr. Kevin Q/C, for the prosecution, now rose and looked the accused straight in the eye. Why, he wanted to know, had not Warren told the police that someone inside the car had grabbed the gun. Warren replied that when he was being interviewed he was confused by events. "I didn't have clear in my own mind what had happened," he excused himself. Mr. Machin referred to the evidence given by the witnesses in Roy Gray's car and queried whether they were wrong when they said that no-one had grabbed the gun. "They must be," replied Warren.

Mr. Machin also questioned if the witnesses were also wrong when they affirmed that Roy Gray had never been involved in any of the fighting at the Grange. Warren was adamant that Gray had kicked him last but was forced to admit that he could not describe his last attacker to the police and he confessed that he thought that he had been clean shaven, whilst it had been pointed out that Roy Gray had a prominent moustache. "Do you now accept that you made a mistake?" Mr Machin demanded. "No sir!" came the unequivocal reply.

Warren did admit to being angry at being beaten up at the club but, despite Mr. Machin's insistence, denied seeking revenge for his humiliation at the Grange that night. He was equally certain that he had not fired the gun but that someone had pulled it.

Resuming his place in the dock the accused had to listen to the prosecution and defence counsel sum up before Mr. Justice Chapman addressed the jury. "Roy Gray was as innocent as a baby in a pram. You may think the case is a pretty ghastly comment on the state of society in which we live to-day. It shows how terrible the situation is when people can treat guns so light-heartedly and go out for no more reason than to have a fight that you have lost and this then finishes with someone on the mortuary slab who was totally innocent."

His lordship commented on the evidence of Wendy Lowe. "Perhaps the best witness of all. 'He (Warren) pulled the trigger. I saw him!' she had said. The occupants of Roy Gray's car had explained what had happened in those dark few seconds in the early hours of that Sunday morning. You will notice that there is no suggestion that it was an accident. No suggestion that he shot at the windscreen. No suggestion of any grappling to try and get hold of the gun." Referring to statements made by Warren to the police, Mr. Justice Chapman further added that Warren disputed that he told the police that he had pointed the gun at Gray.

At the end of the three week trial Warren was found guilty of Roy Gray's murder and was sentenced to life imprisonment. Chamberlain was adjudged to be guilty of manslaughter with a strong recommendation to mercy by the jury. Accordingly, Mr. Justice Chapman placed him on probation for two years.

A DIVISION OF THE SPOILS – DEATH

BUCKINGHAM – 1983

In May 1984, two men were put up in to the dock at Reading Crown Court. One of them, 21 year old Paul Moseley, was charged with the murder of 45 year old Albert George Holloway and additionally with wounding Stephen Holloway, his son, at Buckingham in November of the previous year. His co-accused, Peter Andrew Gibbs, 17, had been charged with the manslaughter of Albert Holloway and with causing actual bodily harm to Colin Holloway, another son of the deceased. Both the defendants pleaded not guilty to the charges and sat down, while the Judge, jury and spectators in the Court listened as the case against the two accused unfolded.

Mr. Paul Focke Q/C rose and, addressing the jury, opened the case for the prosecution. The killing, he commenced, had its origins in May of 1983, when Colin Holloway had broken into a cricket pavilion in Buckingham and had stolen some wine, cigarettes and a barrel of beer. He had been arrested shortly afterwards and, to the annoyance of certain of his friends, had told the investigating Police officers where he had secreted the barrel of beer. Colin later appeared at Court and was duly sentenced for the offence.

It was some months later, went on Mr. Focke, that the two accused went to the Holloway home in Bourton Road, Buckingham, and informed Albert George Holloway that his son, Colin, owed them £50. Reminding them that Colin was serving a period of 'Youth custody' as a result of the burglary, he rather curtly told Moseley and Gibbs to leave. This abrupt dismissal had hardly endeared the Holloways in the eyes of

Bourton Road, Buckingham, where the attack took place.

the two men, and the refusal to hand over what they perceived as their 'cut' still rankled with them.

On Saturday, 26th November 1983, Gibbs and his girl friend Sharon (1) were drinking with two friends in The Mitre public house in Mitre Street, Buckingham, which is situated just out of the town centre, when Paul Moseley turned up. After a few minutes Moseley took Gibbs to one side and had a short conversation with him. When they returned to the small group Moseley turned to Gibbs and allegedly said, "Are you going or not?" Then, turning to the others, he pointedly added, "If anyone asks you, I've been here all night." Mr. Focke paused momentarily and glanced up from his brief at the jury to allow them to appreciate the significance of that remark, before continuing with his opening speech.

One of the girls in the small group then noticed that Moseley had two knives, one up each sleeve, and she saw Gibbs take one of them. Moseley then calmly announced that he intended to kill someone. Moseley, Gibbs and his girl friend then left the Mitre and walked in the direction of Bourton Road, Moseley allegedly repeating that he

The Mitre public house, Buckingham.

was going to kill someone and then asking Gibbs' girl friend if she had ever seen a throat cut. "It just spurts with blood!" he laughed. As the threesome passed a school-yard, the young girl was left behind as the two men walked determinedly on.

A few minutes later, on their arrival at the Holloway home, Moseley demanded £50 from Colin. Albert Holloway told Moseley and Gibbs to leave or he would call the Police. The two men would not be denied what they thought was rightfully theirs, and forced their way into the house. A general free-for-all ensued, with Gibbs fighting Colin Holloway in the front room, whilst Albert Holloway once more ordered Moseley to get out of his house, placing his hands upon the intruder's shoulders to reinforce his command.

It was at this point, went on Mr. Focke, that Moseley took out a knife and thrust it into Albert Holloway's stomach. As Holloway's arms fell from his assailant's shoulders, Moseley stuck the knife into his throat. Albert Holloway collapsed on the floor and Moseley now turned on Stephen Holloway, another son, and commenced slashing at his face.

Albert Holloway, by some super-human endeavour, raised himself from the hall floor and chased Moseley down the front path, only for the roles then to be reversed, with Moseley pursuing Mr. Holloway back up the path to the front of the house. As he passed the front door, Albert fell to the floor once again, and there was a pause in the fray as it was realised that he had been very seriously injured.

An ambulance attended, but it was too late to save Albert Holloway. The Police were also hastily summoned and P.C. Goldsworthy was the first officer to attend. He was told the circumstances of the bloody incident and arrested Gibbs, who had remained at the house. Within minutes other Police officers went to Moseley's flat and, forcing open the door, detained him as well. He denied going to the house in Bourton Road and having anything to do with the death of Albert Holloway.

At the post-mortem examination it was discovered that Holloway had been stabbed five times; the fatal wound had been to the stomach, which had been pierced between two ribs, penetrating the heart and the base of the lung.

Stephen Holloway was now called into the witness box and he gave a graphic account of the confrontation at the house; of how Moseley and Gibbs had burst in and the fight that had broken out between the last named and his brother Colin. He had seen his father grapple with Moseley, who had then pulled a knife from his pocket and had stabbed his father in the stomach and throat. "Then he came at me!" he told the hushed Court. He had turned to go upstairs when he felt a sharp pain to the back of his head. He was later taken to the hospital and had to have nine stitches inserted in the wound that had been inflicted by his attacker. He told of his father chasing Moseley down the path and of being chased back and collapsing. He had dialled 999 for the Ambulance and the Police but, owing to the blood flowing from the wound, he had had trouble making himself understood. While he was telephoning the emergency services, he went on, his father was writhing in agony on the floor. Suddenly, he rolled on his back and stopped breathing.

Gibbs, he continued, had then re-appeared from the front room where he had pursued Colin and, looking down at the body of Albert Holloway, had remarked, "You can't pin this on me. I never did it."

At this point, after hearing from several other witnesses, the prosecution case closed, and the Crown Court adjourned for the week-end. When it resumed, defence counsel called Peter Gibbs, and he walked over to the witness box to give his version of the events of that November night. He recalled that he had been in The Mitre public house with some friends when Paul Moseley arrived. A short time had elapsed before Moseley had called him over and said, "Let's sort Holloway out!" He knew, he told the court, that Moseley was referring to Colin Holloway, adding "I thought he was talking rubbish and I went back and had a drink."

Moseley had then come over to their table and had repeated that he was going to sort Colin out. Moseley had then pulled up his trouser leg and Gibbs had seen a knife pushed down his boot. He alleged that Moseley had two more knives, one up each sleeve, and asked Gibbs to take them but he had declined. "Everyone could see they were there and I eventually took one, because people were looking and it was embarrassing… he was making a scene and I put it in the back pocket of my jeans. I didn't intend to use a knife that night on anyone. I heard Moseley talk about killing someone, but I thought it was absolute rubbish and I didn't think he would do anything like that." They had then left the pub. "I thought…there would be some verbal abuse and the door would be slammed in our face. On the way Moseley had said again that he was going to kill someone, but I didn't believe it for one moment."

On reaching the house in Bourton Road, Moseley had, he related, on encountering the two brothers and their father, mentioned something about money. Colin informed them that he did not want either of the intruders there and had endeavoured to push past his father to get at Moseley. Mr. Holloway had attempted to intervene, Gibbs went on, and had then said that he would telephone the Police. He (Gibbs) had stepped past the front door into the house to see if Mr. Holloway was indeed phoning the Police, when Colin had grabbed him and pushed him up against the wall. A fight had then taken place between the two, which was only interrupted when Stephen Holloway shouted out that his father was dead! I didn't know he was dead but he looked badly injured and I just couldn't leave him. "Moseley," he rather pointedly added, "had just gone."

It was the next day, when the co-accused, Paul Moseley, entered the witness box. He admitted that he had carried a knife in his boot when he arrived at The Mitre that fateful Saturday night, for the reason that he had nowhere else to carry it. He firmly stated that he had no intention of visiting Colin Holloway and he did not have the knife for that purpose.

He had had one drink when Gibbs had asked him to go to the Holloway house because he was owed some money or something. Gibbs had requested his company 'in case they started any violence'.

When they were outside the pub he had mentioned that he had been gutting some rabbits, and Gibbs had asked him if he was carrying a knife with him. When he had replied that he was, Gibbs had taken it from him. "I think it might have been in my sleeve then. There was only one knife and it came from my boot. When it was in my boot it started irritating the back of my ankle...so I took it out and put it up my sleeve," he explained.

Moseley denied that he had requested the group in the pub to give him an alibi by saying that he had been there all night, and with regard to him stating that he was going to kill someone he might have said it but only in fun. "I was in a happy mood, laughing and joking. Peter thought there might be some trouble from the Holloways, but what he was going to do with the knife was his business. If he wasn't going up there to see Colin I wouldn't have gone."

When they had arrived at the house in Bourton Road, Peter had asked if Colin was there, and his brother had emphatically replied,

"No!" Then Colin had appeared with his father. Moseley had made the remark about thinking he was not in when Gibbs had mentioned something about money. There had been some talking and he, Moseley, had started shouting and telling the Holloways to shut up. Colin and his father, he added, had shouted back at him and Colin had either tried to kick or punch him, and a general fight had then commenced. "I saw the blade of a knife waving about and I dived in to try and break it up and I think the father dived in to try and stop it as well." He said that he had been pushed out of the house and the door had been shut on him. It was locked and he could not regain entry. "It seemed rather pointless to try and get back in. I did not realise that anyone had been stabbed or cut or injured with a knife." Later that same night when he had been arrested by the Police on suspicion of murder, his one thought had been, "I just didn't believe them."

When questioned by his barrister as to why he had given Detective Superintendent Diccox, the investigating officer, an untruthful account of what had taken place, he replied that it was because they would not let him see a solicitor. He further denied that he had told anyone that he stabbed Stephen Holloway or his father, and he had not talked to Gibbs about it whilst on remand in Oxford Prison. Under cross-examination Moseley denied that he was suggesting that Gibbs had stabbed Holloway. He also repudiated the evidence of one of the girls in the Mitre pub that he had more than one knife, as he also refuted that it had been Gibbs who did not want to go to the Holloway house.

After the defence and prosecuting counsel had made their addresses and the Judge had summed up, the jury were out for just over six hours with majority 'Guilty' verdicts against Paul Moseley and unanimous verdicts against Peter Gibbs.

Mr. Justice Woolf, in sentencing Moseley to life imprisonment for the murder, commented, "…This was a callous crime that you committed and you have not shown one jot of remorse." A sentence of four years imprisonment was imposed for the wounding charge.

Peter Gibbs was sentenced to two years Youth Custody for the manslaughter and nine months for the assault. Mr. Justice Woolf added,

"I fully accept that you would not be standing where you are now but for Moseley."

(1)   Not her real name.

THE MURDEROUS MILKMAN

LOUDWATER, HIGH WYCOMBE - 1985

To most people, the milkman is a friendly caller at the house, delivering the order, collecting his money, exchanging the time of day, all usually done in a cheery way. If he is lucky, the grateful response of his customers will be a tip at Christmas. A more innocuous occupation it would be difficult to imagine. Yet they are as human as the rest of us and as prone to committing any act, normal or abnormal, as any other citizen.

In 1920 for instance, George Arthur Bailey, a milkman of Little Marlow, placed an advertisement in the Bucks Free Press, requesting young ladies to participate in a musical experiment with him. He then attempted to seduce one of the respondents, after murdering his wife in the same house. Bailey was caught, tried at the Buckinghamshire Assizes, found guilty and ultimately executed (1).

Sixty-five years later, another milkman took the life of a young woman in nearby Loudwater. In 1985, Mrs. Linda Tate had been married to her husband Stephen for just over a year. They lived in a first floor maisonette in Clearbrook Close with their infant son. Stephen worked with Linda's father, Dick Redrup.

One afternoon in July, Mrs. Tate, on hearing a knock at the door, opened it, to be confronted by her milkman, Alan Warwick. He inveigled his way into the maisonette on the pretext that he was collecting the money owed to him. As Mrs. Tate went back upstairs, Warwick followed her, closing the front door behind him. A neighbour of the Tates suddenly heard a long scream come from the upstairs maisonette, followed by a woman shouting "You bastard!" Then all went ominously silent.

Later that same afternoon, Mr. Redrup dropped his son-in-law off at Clearbrook Close. Stephen went indoors, but came running out and blurted out that Linda was dead. Mr. Redrup, fearing that his daughter had had a heart attack, rushed in to see that Linda had been stabbed in the throat and torso. She was quite dead.

When the Police attended, their investigations led them quickly to Warwick. He attempted to explain away the marks to his face by saying that he had been scratched by a rosebush. Pressed on the matter, he confessed that he had killed Linda, telling the detectives who interviewed him that he had purchased a kitchen knife the day prior to the murder from a hardware store. He had then gone to Mrs. Tate and threatened her that, if she did not give him sex, he would harm her with the knife. He showed the detectives where he had hidden the weapon and also the blood stained panties that had belonged to Linda Tate and which he had kept.

Warwick was arrested, charged with Mrs. Tate's murder, and in due course appeared at Reading Crown Court in February 1986, when he pleaded guilty to the crime. His defence counsel, Mr. Phillip Cox Q/C, in mitigation, said in Court that the victim reminded his client, in a vague way, of his wife from whom he was divorced. Mrs. Warwick had been granted a decree nisi on the grounds of her husband's unreasonable behaviour. Mr. Cox related that there had been sexual problems between Warwick and his wife.

The trial Judge, Mr. Justice Allwith, had no hesitation in passing the mandatory sentence of life imprisonment upon Warwick.

(1) For a full account of this murder see, 'Murder in Buckinghamshire', by the author.

BURIED ALIVE!

HIGH WYCOMBE - 1986

In the autumn of 1986, Michael Gausman was uneasy about the activities of a man he had been observing on the Rye, an area of open parkland in the centre of High Wycombe. Michael had been the Parks Warden for the District Council for the previous 14 years and, as his title suggested, patrolled the open spaces in the locality with his German Shepherd dog. If he saw anything untoward as he went round, he would make a note of it. Now he was concerned about one man in particular. Michael had seen him going up to children and chatting to them as they played. At first the man had been dressed in ordinary clothes, but lately Michael had seen him in the uniform of a security guard and wearing a 'walkie-talkie' radio on his hip, and he had apparently been telling the children that he was a Metropolitan Policeman.

Michael decided that the Police ought to be informed, and consequently he called at High Wycombe Police Station and voiced his concern, suggesting that something should be done to curtail the man's activities. As he left the Police Station, Michael considered that he had done his public duty.

Some six months later, on Saturday, 2nd May 1987, 12 year old Martin Butler rose from his bed just after 10 a.m. His father, Terry, just back from a taxi-ing trip to Hounslow, made him a cup of tea. Martin then went out into the back yard and played with a friend of his from next door. He came back indoors to watch a Dr. Who programme on television and afterwards said he was going out. He made his way to the 'Pipes', a lonely short cut used by B.M.X. riders and scramblers.

During the course of the day some women passing by saw Martin sitting alone near a pond by a disused railway line. More ominously, they also noticed a man in his mid-twenties loitering in the area.

Later that evening, whilst Jean, Mrs. Butler's grown-up daughter from a previous marriage, baby-sat, Terry and his wife Carol went out. By 9 p.m., when Martin had not returned home, Jean had become worried and contacted Terry at the Wycombe Marsh Royal British Legion Club. They had assumed that Martin was at the home of one of his friends. The police were informed and immediately a massive search was mounted involving friends of the family and relations, but no trace could be found of the boy that night.

The next morning a man and his young son were in the area, looking for any signs that foxes might be about, when they saw some newly dug earth. As they approached the mound, the man noticed two lifeless arms jutting out. Martin Butler had been found. What had started out as a missing person enquiry was now a murder investigation.

The team of Police officers which now formed the 'murder squad' was led by the late Detective Superintendent Andrew Vallis with Detective Chief Inspector (later Superintendent) Laurie Ekins as second in command, and after they had visited the scene of the killing Martin's body was removed for a post-mortem examination, where it was ascertained that Martin had been subjected to a vicious attack. His assailant had inflicted some really heavy blows to his head, which had resulted in his skull being fractured in several places. Additionally the post-mortem showed that Martin had still been alive when his killer had covered him up with earth, for traces of soil were found in his mouth and larynx.

Extensive enquiries were made by the detectives engaged in the murder enquiry, and nearly all the people who had been in the area during the course of the day were traced and were able to account for themselves. However, there was one person of whom mention was made who could not be found, and his description was placed in a prominent position in the Incident Room, and a Photofit of the unknown man was issued to the press. Still he was not discovered and, although he was convinced that he was a local man, the two senior detectives decided that the murder ought to be given an airing on the B.B.C. programme 'Crimewatch U.K.', which would ask for assistance from the public nation-wide. Although many calls followed, some genuine, some false and even, surprisingly, some that were abusive, none of them advanced the investigation.

It was at a conference with senior officers one day that Chief Inspector Ekins, despite having reservations about staging a reconstruction, persuaded Superintendent Vallis that, if the enquiry was not going to grind to a halt, perhaps one should be held in an effort to trace the mystery man. It was as a result of this that the police were led to a guard working for Burns Security, 21 year old Christopher Stallwood.

Whilst being interviewed by the detectives, he admitted striking Martin with a brick, even when the boy had collapsed on the ground, and had then left him moaning. He, Stallwood, had returned about quarter of an hour later, only to discover that Martin was still breathing. He had

Detective Superintendent Andy Vallis, Senior Investigating Officer.

hit him again and dragged him into some bushes, and had pulled down some earth in an effort to cover him. Stallwood had then, callously, left the boy to die. The reason he gave for his attack on the 12-year-old was that he thought Martin was following him and that he, Stallwood, had lost his temper with him. He was charged with the boy's murder.

Stallwood pleaded not guilty to murder at the Crown Court but guilty to manslaughter by reason of diminished responsibility, the plea being accepted by the Crown Prosecutor, Mr. Jeffrey Burke Q/C. He told the court that the killing was unprovoked and motiveless and that Stallwood was a grave and immediate danger to the public and had a psychopathic disorder. (Even Stallwood's mother admitted in an interview with a local press reporter that he had been subject to tantrums of violent rage throughout his life and had sometimes attacked her and his younger sisters.)

After hearing reports from a consultant psychiatrist that Stallwood was a dangerous man and that there was a risk of his committing further offences should he remain at large, the Judge, Sir Laurence Verney,

Detective Superintendent Vallis in the Incident Room.

commenting that he was satisfied on the evidence before the court that Stallwood was suffering from a psychopathic disorder, ordered him to be detained without limitation of time for the protection of the public.

THE MURDERER HAD A HAMMER TOE

BLEDLOW RIDGE – 1987

One of the most picturesque places in mid – Bucks is Bledlow Ridge. High up, one can walk the Ridgeway path whilst looking over the Buckinghamshire countryside where it adjoins Oxfordshire. At any time of the year it can be exhilarating and, despite the presence of passing traffic, it can also be quite lonely. It is perhaps the loneliness that regularly attracts courting couples, with various spots suitable for their assignations; unfortunately it has also proved ideal for murder!

*

In August of 1987 Rachael Partridge was just seventeen years of age, still living with her parents at a farm in nearby Chinnor Hill. She worked at a dental laboratory in the town and was planning to travel to Italy shortly with her boyfriend.

On Tuesday, August 25th she finished work and went to a friend's house where she stayed until 7p.m. She then telephoned her mother who came and collected her. Rachael asked if she would take her into Thame but Mrs. Partridge refused as her husband needed the car for a village meeting that night, the family's other car having been written off in an accident the week previously. After a dispute over this, Rachael asked to be dropped off in Chinnor so that she could thumb a lift into Thame. This Mrs. Partridge dutifully did.

A workmate then noticed Rachael, picked her up and took her to the house of another of her friends in Croft Road, Thame, where, in preparation for her forthcoming holiday, Rachael spent some time on her friend's sun bed. At approximately 8.30 p.m. she left, her intention

The picturesque view from Bledlow Ridge.

being to hitch a lift back to her home at Chinnor Hill.

Mr. and Mrs. Partridge were not too concerned when Rachael did not return that night as she had stayed at friends' homes overnight before. However, when she had not shown up next morning, they became alarmed and decided that they ought to report her missing to the police.

Just a few minutes before they made this decision, a farm worker, Richard Warry and the fifteen year old son of his employer, had been driving along on a tractor in Wigans Lane, Bledlow Ridge when they noticed something lying at the entrance to a barn. Stopping the tractor, Mr. Warry got down to see what it could be. At first, as he approached, he thought it was either a tailor's dummy or an inflatable doll, but as he moved closer he could see that it was the almost naked body of a young girl. Both Mr. Warry and the youth rushed to the nearby Callow Down Farm and reported the matter to the farmer's wife who in turn contacted the police.

The first police officer on the scene was Detective Inspector, later Superintendent, Barry Prendergast who, fortuitously, happened to be in

Along the lane where murder took place.

the area on another assignment when the message regarding the found body was transmitted from Thames Valley Police Headquarters. It was quickly established that the body was that of the missing girl Rachael Partridge and it was seen that she had been brutally put to death.

Detective Superintendent Roy Payne was placed in charge of the investigation into the murder of Rachael, with Detective Inspector Prendergast as his second in command. Scenes of Crimes Officers and a Home Office pathologist attended the barn where the young girl's body lay. Rachael had been subjected to a fierce attack; she had been sexually assaulted, her jaw had been broken, either by being thrown against or struck by a piece of metal, before being strangled by her attacker placing his arm around her neck and crushing the life out of her. Her clothing, apart from a pair of socks that she was still wearing when she had been found, had all been removed.

An Incident Room was immediately set up at High Wycombe Police Station and teams of detectives began the search for Rachael's murderer. Her boyfriend had, of necessity, to be interrogated regarding not only his relationship with Rachael but also his movements during the crucial time that she was missing.

Meanwhile, at the barn where Rachael's body had been found, the Scenes of Crimes Officers went methodically about their work. Tyre marks were found which were similar to those used on a Morris Marina; a stockinged footmark was discovered, showing that the person responsible had a hammer toe and, during a post-mortem performed on Rachael, pieces of 'Celotex', a special insulating foam, were found in her hair. All pieces in an intricate jigsaw puzzle building up a case against an eventual accused person.

Police also appealed to those courting couples who had used the Bledlow Ridge for their romantic trysts, whether legal or otherwise, to come forward under a promised cloak of secrecy, in an effort to see if any light could be thrown on to the crime.

One of the peculiar things that arose during the enquiry occurred on the day after the finding of the body when a telephone call was received by the mother of a friend of Rachael's stating that the caller had got her daughter! Actually she was safe and sound in her own house, but the police were quickly informed of the weird call and they took it most seriously at the time, although eventually it was realised that it was a cruel hoax that had been perpetrated.

Another matter that concerned the police was the fact that young people were still hitching lifts in the Chinnor area, despite what had taken place and the fact that Rachael's killer was still at large. "It's absolutely crazy!" one police officer exploded to the press, before advising potential hitchhikers to let their parents or friends give them a lift to their destination. "But don't thumb lifts!" he earnestly advised.

Snippets of information came into the Incident Room; Rachael had been seen talking to a man in a Morris Marina at a roundabout in Thame; a Ford Fiesta van had been seen in the area where Rachael's body had been found; two hitchhikers had been given a lift by a local woman on the night of the murder and an appeal for them to come forward was made. Rachael was a follower of a local pop group and, therefore, other fans were also sought. All this information had to be thoroughly investigated along with other strands of enquiries, and it all took time.

Late summer turned to autumn and then to winter as the enquiry ground remorselessly on. In an effort to remind the public that the killer was still at large, posters with a recent photograph of Rachael were distributed to shops, garages and other premises in the Chinnor area. The police carried out stop checks on vehicles and passers-by to ascertain if they could add anything to help clear up the mystery.

Appeals were placed on the B.B.C.'s programme, 'Crimewatch U.K.', and as a result a number of calls came into the studio and the Incident Room. One, which seemed very promising, came from a lachrymose caller who said that she had seen Rachael hitching from the Thame roundabout on the night she had been murdered, adding that she had later seen her get into a white car near Chinnor Hill. She then rang off and Nick Ross, the presenter of the programme, pleaded with her to contact the police with her vital information. At midnight she telephoned the Incident Room still crying. Superintendent Payne stated that the police would investigate the information given and that they were taking the call most seriously. Eventually, it was discovered to be just another hoax and the police officers' thoughts at the waste of time and manpower spent on this can be imagined. What must go through a person's mind to perpetrate a cruel trick like this?

During this time, as a matter of course, a trawl of the Local Intelligence Officer's records was being carried out and several men who had past convictions for violence and indecency came into the 'frame' and were interviewed. Samples of their blood were taken and submitted to the forensic scientists for comparison with the semen obtained from Rachael's body. D.N.A. was in its infancy and great care was needed that the analysis was correct, and therefore it seemed ages before the 'Murder Team' at High Wycombe was apprised of the conclusion. One of the six hundred men interviewed at the police station several weeks before and from whom a blood sample had been taken was the perpetrator!

*

It was at 5.23 a.m. on Thursday, 21st January 1988 that Detective Sergeant Jones confronted the prime suspect, Ronald Cheshire, at his home at Gawcott near Buckingham. When the Detective Sergeant informed him that he was under arrest, Cheshire's response was "You have got to be joking!" He should have known that the police never jest about anything as serious as murder.

Cheshire was placed in the rear of the police car and conveyed to High Wycombe Police Station. "Why have you picked on me?" he enquired. "I have done some pretty stupid things in my life but not silly things like that. I've got loads of friends to say I never left Buckingham," adding that he had never met or indeed known Rachael Partridge.

Cheshire was told that the reason for his arrest was that his blood sample matched the samples of semen obtained from Rachael's body. His immediate reaction was that the police had got it wrong, but the detectives travelling with him in the car asked why it was then that the blood samples he had given matched the sample of semen. Cheshire was silenced by this information and maintained this attitude until they had almost reached High Wycombe. "How can they tell if it is mine?" he enquired. Detective Sergeant Jones patiently explained the technique to him and Cheshire mulled this over. "Did you have sex with her?" the detective asked. "Possibly," he replied, adding that he had originally picked her up as she was standing outside Thame Town Hall.

On his arrival at the police station Cheshire was formally interrogated by detectives. He had been on foot, he told them, when he had seen Rachael standing by the Town Hall in Thame. They had chatted and had then gone for a walk and had arranged to meet two days later by the Town Hall once again. He admitted that he had had sexual intercourse with Rachael but she had been a willing participant. It had taken place in his van at Thame Cattle Market, he added.

The detectives then asked him how he was so sure that the girl he had been with had also been the murder victim. "I'm not really sure. She never said her name. She didn't tell me where she lived and I didn't see her again," he replied.

He still maintained that he had not had intercourse with Rachael on the night that she had been murdered, but when the police reminded him that his semen had been found in her body and that intercourse must have taken place on that fateful night, Cheshire admitted that he must have done. But he denied going to Callow Down Farm, Bledlow Ridge, with her.

The interviewing detectives pointed out that they knew that he had been at the barn where Rachael's body had been found because the tyre marks found there matched those on his van. He also had a hammer-toe and the impression of his stockinged footmark at the scene indicated that the murderer also had that deformity; furthermore, fragments of a special insulating foam found in Rachael's hair matched the foam used at the garage where Cheshire worked.

Confronted with this, Cheshire chose to amend his story once more. He and Rachael had had intercourse at a turn off along the Thame-Chinnor road. They had then talked about his banger racing and about her forthcoming holiday. Rachael had then suggested that they go to a barn at Callow Down Farm where they had carried on chatting. They had not, Cheshire maintained, had intercourse there. Afterwards he had dropped her off at Gooseneck on Chinnor Hill, a quiet isolated spot along Wigans Lane popular with C.B. radio enthusiasts, and less than a mile from her house. He had then, he calmly told detectives, gone home.

The police considered that they had enough evidence and Cheshire was now charged with Rachael Partridge's murder.

*

It was over a year later, in March 1989, that Cheshire stood trial at Reading Crown Court. Pleading not guilty to murder, he sat down between two prison officers and listened to the evidence as it unfolded against him.

He heard two witnesses say that they had seen a van drive off along Wigans Lane just before midnight on the night in question, the driver hiding his face as he passed by. The police, during their intensive enquiries, had also traced four C.B. enthusiasts who had been at Gooseneck during that night, but neither could recall seeing Cheshire's van nor seeing Rachael. Cheshire's boss and fellow workmates informed the court that they used Celotex foam and had placed a sheet of it in the back of Cheshire's van in an effort to cut out the engine noise. It was still there after the murder had taken place, although Cheshire consistently denied that he had any Celotex in his vehicle.

When the forensic scientists stated that the chances of the semen found in Rachael's body not coming from the accused were somewhat less than one in ten and a half million, Cheshire's fate was sealed.

After a five and a half day trial, the jury deliberated for ninety minutes before returning with a unanimous verdict of guilty.

The judge wasted little time on the accused. "You have been convicted of this brutal and tragic crime on evidence which was very clear." After passing the only sentence that the law allowed, life imprisonment, the prison officers gripped hold of a shaken Cheshire as they took him away to gaol.

When interviewed by the press after the trial, Cheshire's father was forthright. "It was the right sentence and a fair verdict!"

INDEX

INDEX

INDEX

122, 123, 124, 125, 126, 128
Milton Keynes 104, 116, 118
Mitre, The, public house 137, 140, 141, 142
Money Savings Stores 48
Moody, Mrs. 33, 34, 35, 36, 37, 38, 39, 41, 43, 45
    Moody, Mr. 37
Morris Marina 154
    Minor 130, 131, 132
Moseley, Paul 136, 137, 138, 139, 140, 141, 142, 143
Mullan, Thomas 78
Municipal Corporations Act 28
'Murder Team' 155
N
Nash Lee Road 97, 100
National Viewers & Listeners Assoc. 118
'navvies' 47
Newport Pagnell 47, 48, 49, 50, 51
New Scotland Yard 89, 91
'Nora' 70
Norman, Mrs. 101
Norman Conquest of England 47
Norsemen 47
Northern Ireland 104
North Wales 103
O
Old Stratford 104
Olley, Richard 14
Omega watch 86
Ostrich Inn 1, 2, 3, 4, 5
Ouse, River 47

Owen, Mr. John, Q/C 116
Oxfordshire 47, 151
P
Page, Barrie 80, 81, 82, 83, 84, 85, 86, 87, 88, 89, 90, 91, 93, 94, 96
Palmerston, Lord 27
Parnell 49
Parrott, William 59
Parslow, Genevieve 98, 99, 101
Partridge, Mr. 152
    Mrs. 151, 152
    Rachael 151, 152, 153, 154, 155, 156, 157, 158
Paull, Mr. Justice 77
Payne, Det. Supt., Roy 153, 155
'Peirce' Mrs. Kathy 55
Perkins, Dr. J. 76
Perkins, Samuel, Sergeant 13, 14, 16, 24, 25
Phillip, King of France 1
'Photofit' 147
'Pipes', the 146
Police 45
    '5' television programme 85
    North Riding of Yorkshire 128
    Thames Valley 122, 128, 153
Police Stations; Aylesbury 98, 101
    Chesham 76
    Harrow Road 69
    High Wycombe 73, 146, 153, 156
    Marlow 123, 124, 127
    Slough 66, 71, 84, 87, 91, 94, 132

INDEX

INDEX

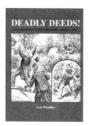

BUCKINGHAMSHIRE MURDERS

DEADLY DEEDS!

THE LAST PATROL

Len Woodley

Three books by Len Woodley each dealing with murder.

Buckinghamshire Murders contains thoroughly researched accounts of seventeen murders ranging across the old County of Buckinghamshire. Commencing from the early nineteenth century right up to modern times. Amongst others you will read about the Newton Longville shop-keeper murdered for a few shillings; the Dagnall killer; murders for no apparent reason at Buckingham and Denham; the unsolved murder of the canal man at Slough; love affairs that went tragically wrong at Burnham and Bourne End; a fatal ambush at Botolph Claydon.

Deadly Deeds includes accounts of fourteen murders that have occurred within the County of Buckinghamshire, plus one from central Europe. You will read about the Victorian 'Quaker' who, having escaped the gallows once, faced them again some years later; the country squire killed walking home from church; the gypsy who robbed and killed an old man, and the husband who shot his wife and her lover in one county, was tried in another and executed in yet another.

The Last Patrol details Policemen killed on duty by a criminal act within the area now covered by the Thames valley Police – namely the counties of Berkshire, Buckinghamshire and Oxfordshire. These Police officers all started on their last day of duty as though they were going out on normal Police work, not one gave a thought to the possibility that he might be involved in, or sent to, a life-threatening job.

Book Castle
PUBLISHING

BLETCHLEY PARK'S SECRET SISTERS
Psychological Warfare in World War 11

John A. Taylor

Bletchley Park will be forever associated with the secret intelligence activities of World War Two. Yet in addition to the incredible achievements of the code breakers, only a few miles away several other secret organisations were also achieving clandestine success, with operations that were conducted from centres hidden in the local countryside. This region had been chosen by the Government because it was remote from the London Blitz yet still maintained good road and rail communications with the Capital - but what did these secret organisations do?

In a highly subversive campaign, propaganda played an early and effective role, selecting recruits from amongst the refugees fleeing Nazi oppression. Gathered in large, local houses, there they would write and rehearse propaganda scripts for radio broadcasts to enemy territory. At a secret studio, these broadcasts were then recorded onto discs and taken by the Secret Service to radio transmitting stations, hidden in the local countryside.

Under the control of the Communications Section of the Secret Intelligence Service, another radio station transmitted decoded information from Bletchley Park to Allied military commanders overseas. Further radio stations maintained contact with secret agents, sent on missions deep inside Occupied Europe. In hidden workshops, advanced radio equipment for their use was designed and manufactured and in various country houses specialised training schools were set up.

Later in the war, not far from Woburn Abbey an ultra modern recording and broadcast studio was then built which, when linked to the most powerful radio transmitter in Europe, began use in sophisticated operations that would completely deceive and confuse the Germans.

This book now tells the little known story of all these other secret activities, the fascinating story of Bletchley Park's 'Secret Sisters'.

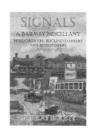

SIGNALS: A RAILWAY MISCELLANY

Murray Eckett

Since the dawn of the railway age, a fascinating mixture of lines have criss-crossed the counties of Hertfordshire, Buckinghamshire, and Bedfordshire. They range from narrow gauge examples, such as the Leighton Buzzard Narrow Gauge Railway and Whipsnade Zoo's "Jumbo Express", constructed for both commercial and tourism purposes, to main trunk routes. Such lines commence at London's Kings Cross, Euston and St Pancras stations, that first came to public attention during the glorious era of steam and which remain as steadfast today, solid planks within the modern railway network. This book also features some that have survived closure scares, and which remain in use. The most well known lines of this type are the "Abbey Flyer" route between Watford Junction and St Albans Abbey, and that between Bedford and Bletchley. There are others that have fallen before the march of the internal combustion engine, but which live on as public footpaths, accessible to all, prominent amongst these being the former lines between Wolverton and Newport Pagnell, and Watford to Rickmansworth. A number of heritage railway centres and museums are also described, each with their own special characteristics, for example the long lived Buckinghamshire Railway Centre. The story is also told of one of the longest-lived national organisations catering for the "gricer", this being the Locomotive Club of Great Britain. A fascinating selection of photographs add a further dimension to this treasure-trove of the railway world, past and present.